Legal Almanac Series No. 29

LAW FOR
THE
BUSINESSMAN

by Bernard D. Reams, Jr., J. D.
Assistant Professor of Law
Washington University

1974 OCEANA PUBLICATIONS, INC.
Dobbs Ferry, New York

This is the twenty-ninth in a series of LEGAL ALMANACS
which bring you the law on various subjects in nontechnical
language. These books do not take the place of your attorney's
advice, but they can introduce you to your legal rights and responsibilities.

Library of Congress Cataloging in Publication Data

Reams, Bernard D
    Law for the businessman.

    (Legal almanac series, no. 29)
    1. Business law--United States.   I. Title.
K F889.6.R4   346'.73'065   74-8901
ISBN 0-379-11095-4

Manufactured in the United States of America

To Rosemarie Bridget

TABLE OF CONTENTS

INTRODUCTION

In the footsteps of the country's frontiersmen came the early businessman, the craftsman, and the merchant who began the first American commercial establishments that have grown into this nation's industrial, technological, and economic strength. From those early days the importance of small business has been recognized. George Washington said he would "give every encouragement in my power to the manufactures of my country." Small business continues to be a vital part of the United States, basic to its free, independent enterprise system and to the well-being of the entire economy. New and small businesses continue to take root and to grow, increasing at a net rate of 100,000 units each year. There are now some eight million small businesses - 95 percent of all businesses - the bread-winner for one hundred million Americans.

The operation of small business still remains a complex and often precarious undertaking. One need only consult the latest edition of the <u>Statistical Abstract of the United States</u> to learn that literally thousands of businesses, for the most part small ones, fail each year. Several primary reasons exist for this phenomenon. Undoubtedly, the increasing concentration of this nation's commerce and industry in the hands of the conglomerate has had great effect. Small businesses frequently find it difficult, if not impossible, to meet the competition of such economic giants. In addition, inadequate capital for the needs of the business is without question the greatest single cause for the high percentage of bankruptcy or insolvency among the many new business enterprises launched each year.

Perhaps the next most significant reason for failure is the lack of sufficient knowledge or information on the part of the proprietor, or the inability successfully to apply to the business the knowledge and information which is available. The rules and regulations governing the conditions under which large and small businesses alike must operate have become increasingly complex and intricate. With increasing economic and social legislation even the smallest shopkeeper must consider

1

the effect upon his business of income tax regulations, Federal wage and price controls, workmen's compensation requirements, occupational health and safety rules, among many others. Calvin Coolidge said that the business of America is business. To succeed in this venture, one must know, understand, and properly apply the ever changing "rules of the game," -- our laws.

This volume attempts to introduce the reader to the law, but at all times in the context of the practical everyday problems which most new or small businessmen must inevitably face. Theoretical matters or legal principles which have only occasional application are not included. It is the objective of this work to focus on the usual and the practical.

Any book of this type must be used with intelligence and discretion. The discussion presented is necessarily general, and no one should accept as final the answers he finds herein to his own particular problems. The results in the application of general legal principles will vary greatly depending upon the particular facts and circumstances involved. In addition, laws are constantly in flux in a rapidly changing economy, resulting in new statutes and court decisions. Therefore, in any specific situation, professional legal advice and guidance should be sought.

While this work is definitely not intended to enable anyone to dispense with or disregard assistance of an attorney, it is hoped that, in addition to providing a basic background of pertinent information, it will prove useful in two other ways: first, to signal for the reader some situations in which professional advice should be obtained; and second, to aid him in understanding and intelligently applying to his business the advice given. Finally, a word of caution: any attorney will confirm that he can be much more useful if his client will consult him before -- not after -- taking action. For the average businessman motivated by profit, such a policy will prove cheaper in the long run.

Chapter 1

SELECTING THE BUSINESS FORMAT

Organizing the Business

One of the paramount matters which must be settled once the nature of the business and its location have been decided, is the actual form of business organization to be used. As a practical matter, however, nearly all small business is done in only one of three forms: individual ownership or proprietorship, partnership, or corporation. Other alternatives exist for carrying on business, such as the business trust and the joint stock company, but they are met infrequently and are not discussed herein. Thus, each of these three major forms has its advantages and disadvantages, and these matters must be carefully weighed and considered before a final decision is reached.

Many lawyers assume an initial presumption against incorporation in the early stages of a business venture. The corporate form of doing business is probably inadvisable for a small new undertaking as the cost of the privilege of limited liability will probably prove excessive. In addition there is the expense of creating and maintaining a corporation which a sole proprietor would not have to pay. Further, there exists the possibility of serious tax disadvantages. Consider, for one, the double tax on corporate income distributed as dividends; once taxed to the corporation, it is again taxed against the stockholder, making the corporate form of doing business basically unattractive. The corporate form is made appealing for the small business venture only when it can take advantage of the exceptions and unusual provisions in the law.

In weighing all the alternatives available, one must realistically consider the results should one's venture prove unsuccessful. A corporation that fails may bring unsatisfactory tax consequences to the stockholder and place him in a worse posture than if he had not incorporated. Ordinarily, the losses incurred by an individual carrying on a business as a sole proprietor or partner are deductible from his other income. Losses realized by a corporation are of no benefit to it unless in a five-year period it makes profits that offset its losses. An exception, however, exists under I.R.C. §§1371-1377 (otherwise known as the Technical Amendment Act of 1958), and under some states' tax laws where the stockholders of a corporation that qualifies as a "small business" have the option, by following the procedures outlined therein, of being taxed as partnerships. This Act defines a small business corporation as a domestic corporation which is not a member of an affiliated group (as defined in section 1504), and which does not: (1) have more than 10 shareholders; (2) have as a shareholder a person (other than an estate) who is not an individual; (3) have a nonresident alien as a shareholder; and (4) have more than one class of stock.

By 26 U.S.C.A. §1372 (c) popularly known as Subchapter S, an election under subsection (a) may be made by a small business corporation for any taxable year at any time during the first month of such taxable year, or at any time during the month preceding such first month. If such an election is available the substantial tax objection to incorporation will prove moot. If the corporation's loss manifests itself through the liquidation of the corporation or by a stockholder's sale of his shares, his loss will commonly be treated as a capital loss unless it qualifies as a small business loss under I.R.C. §1244 where it is deductible as an ordinary loss. If the loss does not fall within this exception, then it must be applied first against capital gains with the balance being deducted from ordinary income at the rate of $1,000 per year.

Thus, it may prove advisable to start a new business venture as a sole proprietorship or as a partnership until the earning capacity of the business is firmly established. Generally, conversion to a corporate form can later be obtained in a tax-free transaction. As a general rule of thumb when considering the form a business should assume, remember: when in doubt, do not incorporate. Putting assets into a corporation in a tax-free transfer is much easier than getting them out of a corporation without the tax obligation.

The Sole Proprietorship

The oldest, simplest and most prevalent form of business organization is the "sole proprietorship." According to the Statistical Abstract of the United States, of an estimated 12,021,000 business enterprises in the United States in 1969, some 9,430,000 were classified as individual proprietorships. Under this type of operation, one individual owns and manages the business and takes all financial burdens and risks upon himself. He is his own boss and is responsible only to himself. All profits made belong solely to him. At the same time, any losses incurred are his sole responsibility. As the sole proprietor is in business for himself, the legal ramifications in connection with the commencement or termination of his business activities, as well as in connection with actual operations, are generally simpler than those involved in other forms of business enterprises.

The individual proprietorship can be organized informally, involves few problems of control and management, and is generally subject to minimal government regulation. The individual proprietorship, however, ceases to exist on the retirement or death of the proprietor. The advantages for this business format are that it is freely transferable. Ordinarily, this proprietorship is taxed as an individual. Although the sole proprietorship is not a form of business association, it can easily become one by being incorporated, or by admitting others to the business, which is done when creating a partnership.

While these are important considerations, particularly for small businesses, there are also concurrent disadvantages. For example, the obtaining of credit by the individual proprietor is limited by his own solvency. Perhaps the paramount disadvantage is that the sole proprietor assumes all the risks involved. As legal matter, his risk is not limited to the money he has actually invested in the business. Should this business fail or be unable to pay its debts, the creditors have a claim not only against the business itself and the money invested in it, but against any and all property or assets of any sort that the proprietor may own. This includes, for example, his automobile, his personal bank account, as well as other properties. An additional important disadvantage of a sole proprietorship is the severe limitation that is put upon expansion of such a business, particularly when the owner's capital is relatively small.

Clearly, the sole proprietorship is not a form of operation to be used by the individual who wishes to limit the amount of his risk involved in a particular business. Similarly, the sole proprietorship is generally an inadvisable form whenever the business venture is a rather risky or unstable one, or is

5

relatively new and untried. In such situations, the person going into business will be well advised to attempt to limit his undertaking in the business, and that cannot be legally accomplished if the sole proprietorship form of operation is used.

For these reasons, many individuals who engage in business by themselves do not use the sole proprietorship form of organization. Such persons will frequently incorporate their businesses, even though they are actually the sole owners.

The Partnership

A partnership can be defined as an association of two or more persons to carry on, as co-owners, a business for profit. It is in effect a form of individual ownership in which two or more persons are the owners of the business. A true partnership is described as the association of two or more persons, with the legal capacity to be partners, carrying on a business (more than a single venture; the existence of a business purpose) as co-owners for profit. Rules establishing the criteria for a partnership are codified by statute in four-fifths of American jurisdictions with many states adopting the Uniform Partnership Act.

Certain natural advantages are offered by the partnership format of doing business, over that of a sole proprietorship. Generally, a business may be operated more efficiently when two or more individuals share in its management, rather than when all of the problems are in the hands of a single person. More important, however, from the financial point of view, is that the capital involved will ordinarily have been supplied by each of the partners, and in all likelihood there will be more funds available for the business than there might normally be if each of the partners had operated by himself. Similarly, if credit is required, a partnership generally will enjoy better credit relationships than a sole proprietorship since there are additional persons to whom creditors can look for security on the loan. Statistically, partnerships represent a significant alternative to the business corporation with its size varying from two partners to over a hundred partners representing all types of business ventures. Of an estimated 12,021,000 business enterprises in the United States in 1969, 921,000 were listed as partnerships as compared with 1,670,000 corporations.

The principal advantages of the partnership over the corporate form of business enterprise are many. With the general partnership there exists a simplicity of organization. The general partnership agreement exists between the parties and need not be filed with the Secretary of State or recorded in the recorder's office. No organization tax need be paid, no corporate seal purchased, no stock certificates printed, no stock subscriptions obtained, no stockholders' or directors' meetings held. A partnership is not subject to an excess profits tax, if any. It may transact business more freely across state lines, normally without first being licensed to do so. While a partnership is required to file an information income tax return, it pays no tax. Therefore, there is no double income taxation as there is in the case of the corporation where the corporation pays a tax as well as the individuals who receive dividends from the corporation. Finally, the partnership is not subject to taxes on accumulation of surplus imposed by I.R.C. §§ 531-537.

Partnerships are of two basic types: the general partnership and the limited partnership. A general partnership consists of two or more individuals, all of whom are general partners with full status, such as unlimited personal liability and managerial control, and may be formed with little or no statutory formality. Although the general partnership may arise informally, it is sound practice to define the relationships among the partners in a written partnership agreement or articles of partnership. A sample agreement appears as Appendix E. This partnership agreement usually specifies the names of the partnership and its partners, the date of the agreement, the purposes of the partnership, the location and duration of the business, investment of each partner whether in realty, services, personality or cash, any loans to the partnership, the partners' sharing of profits and losses, any remuneration for services, voting and management powers as well as provisions for arbitration of disagreements, voluntary and compulsory retirement, methods of sale or purchase of a deceased or retiring partnership interest with methods for establishing value, possible cross-insurance, duties of all partners, accounting periods and access to books, banking arrangements and authority to sign checks, hiring and discharging of employees, fixing of salaries and wages, etc.

Since a partnership can only result from contract, any party who is capable of entering into a contract may be a partner in a general partnership. Absent any agreement to the contrary, general partners have an equal voice in the management and control of the partnership. A general mutuality exists among all of the partners. The partnership is liable for the wrongful acts and omissions of any of the partners acting in the ordinary course of business to the same extent as the individual wrongdoing partner. It is accountable for the breaches of trust committed by a partner apparently acting within the scope of his authority. Thus, the act of every partner within the apparent scope of the partnership business binds the partnership unless the individual with whom a partner is dealing has knowledge of the fact that the partner involved has no authority to engage in the following activities, and all persons dealing with the partners are charged with knowledge of his lack of authority: 1) assign partnership property in trust for creditors or on the assignee's promise to pay the debts of the partnership; 2) dispose of the good will of the business; 3) perform any act that would make it impossible to carry on the ordinary and normal business of the partnership; 4) confess a judgment; or 5) submit a partnership claim or liability to arbitration or reference.

There are serious drawbacks to this form of business. Just as with the individual proprietorship, there is no limit on the risk which each of the partners takes. Legally, each partner has an unlimited liability for all of the debts of the business. Of course, among themselves, each partner is only responsible for his own share, and he can therefore look to his own partners to share in such debts. But insofar as outside creditors are concerned, there is no limitation on responsibility whatsoever. Thus, where a partnership is composed of two persons who have contributed equally to the partnership and that partnership fails, between themselves each partner is responsible for one-half of the debts. If it should happen, however, that one partner is personally insolvent whereas the other partner is not, the creditors of the business could look to the solvent partner to pay all of the business debts. He could then attempt to collect one-half from his partner, but under the circumstances, he probably would be unable to do so.

There is always present in partnership situations the possibility of disagreement among the partners especially without a written partnership agreement. There may be dissatisfaction as to the sharing of the profits, or with the work to be done by each partner, and so forth. Legally, a partnership

8

can be terminated at any time by any of the partners. Thus, if there is such a disagreement, even though the partnership business is flourishing, any one of the partners can cause the business to end. Under such circumstances, the monies which are likely to be realized on the sale or other disposition of the business are not ordinarily as great as they would be if the partnership business was terminated normally.

Another basic difficulty with both individual proprietorships and with partnerships is that there is no guarantee of continuity of the business. When any one partner dies, for example, the partnership automatically terminates legally. While arrangements may be made in partnership agreements for continuing the business with his heirs, or for the purchase of the business by the remaining partners, these situations cause legal complications and may result in financial loss or other hardships as a result of this stress situation. In conclusion, the dissolution of a partnership can take place in seven different ways:

    1 - by provisions of the articles or partnership agreement;
    2 - by will of all the partners;
    3 - by an act of one or more of the partners alone;
    4 - by a change of the partnership;
    5 - by death of one of the partners;
    6 - by bankruptcy;
    7 - or, by a decree of a court in equity.

The Limited Partnership

A limited partnership is a partnership consisting of one or more general partners and one or more special limited partners who have little managerial control and a limited liability. This organization is a statutory creation formed by two or more individuals under a limited partnership statute which is generally the Uniform Limited Partnership Act adopted in some seven-eighths of the states. In a limited partnership situation, the status of the one or more general partners is substantially identical to that of the two or more general partners in a general partnership. The limited partner's status does differ from that of the general partner in the following significant manner: 1) the liability of each limited partner is restricted to his agreed-upon contribution; 2) the limited partner should not participate in the control of the business; 3) the limited partner may contribute money or other property, but not services; 4) at time of liquidation, each limited partner has priority over the general partner or partners in distribution of net assets.

Certain advantages exist for establishing a business in the limited format. By admitting a limited partner one can attract additional capital to the partnership without any risk of liability on the investor. In the alternative, a limited partner may object to his lack of control in the partnership affairs in order to protect his investment while wanting to avoid liability that may result from any active control on his part of the partnership business. Realistically, any potential investor in a limited partnership must be prepared to have great personal faith in the general partners before he will be inclined to advance capital to the venture.

The Uniform Limited Partnership Act contains several circumstances which can make a limited partner liable to partnership creditors as a general partner. These are: first, when the surname of a limited partner appears in the partnership name and such surname is not also the surname of a general partner or prior to the time that the limited partner became such, the business had been carried on under the name in which his surname appeared or, second, when the limited partner takes part in the control of the business. It should also be noted that some liability may arise as to the limited partner for any false statements made in the certificate. To avoid liability, the limited partner is required to exercise good faith at all times.

The limited partnership requires certain formalities of organization as prescribed by statute. These include filing and sometimes publication of a limited partnership certificate. This certificate includes the following information: name of the partnership; character of the business; location of the principal place of business; the name and place of residence of each member with general and limited partners being respectively designated; the term the partnership is to exist; the amount of cash and a description of, and the agreed value of the other property contributied by each limited partner; any additional contributions, if any, agreed to be made by each limited partner and the times at which or events on the happening of which they shall be made; the time, if agreed upon when the contribution of each limited partner is to be returned; the share of profits or the other compensation by way of income which each limited partner shall receive by reason of his contribution; the

10

right, if given, of a limited partner to substitute an assignee as contributor in his place, and the terms and conditions of the substitution; the right, if given, of the partners to admit additional limited partners; the right, if given, of one or more of the limited partners to priority over other limited partners, as to contributions or as to compensation by way of income, and the nature of such priority.

Certain characteristics of the limited partnership exist as controlled by statute. Generally, a limited partner can demand return of his capital on six month's notice; each limited partner's share of the profits are set forth in the filed certificate with losses generally shared in the same proportion; if a limited partner does not take in administration of the business, his liability is restricted to the amount of his capital investment; the limited partner can assign his interest in capital and profits but cannot substitute the assignee as a limited partner without consent of the other partners; withdrawal of a limited partner does not necessarily force dissolution of the partnership.

The Corporation

The business corporation is a major institution in the contemporary American free enterprise system. Of all methods available for undertaking a business venture, in terms of capital and business, this form is numerically the least significant. Of an estimated 12,021,000 business enterprises in this country in 1969, only 1,670,000 were listed as corporations. These corporations range in size from a one-man, one-shareholder corporation to the conglomerate giants of industry such as General Motors and American Telephone and Telegraph, Co., with their thousands of stockholders.

At law, a corporation is regarded as an artificial person or being, endowed by statute with the capacity of perpetual succession. It is a body created by law composed of individuals united under a common name. Basically statutory in form, its fundamental characteristic is its existence as a separate entity -- it is a being which is separate from its stockholders. One of the best definitions of a corporation was expounded in 1819 by Justice Marshall in the famous Dartmouth College case:

A corporation is an artificial being, invisible, intangible, and existing only in contemplation of law. Being the mere creature of law, it possesses only

11

those properties which the charter of its creation confers upon it, either expressly, or as incidental to its very existence. These are such as are supposed best calculated to effect the object for which it was created. Among the most important are immortality, and if the expression may be allowed, individuality; properties, by which a perpetual succession of many persons are considered as the same, and may act as a single individual. They enable a corporation to manage its own affairs, and to hold property without the perplexing intricacies, or the hazardous and endless necessity of perpetual conveyances for the purpose of transmitting it from hand to hand. It is chiefly for the purpose of clothing bodies of men, in succession, with these qualities and capacities, that corporations were invented, and are in use. By these means, a perpetual succession of individuals are capable of acting for the promotion of the particular object, like one immortal being. The Trustees of Dartmouth College v. Woodward 17 U.S. (4 Wheat.) 518 (1819) at p. 636.

The term "incorporate" can be defined as meaning to create a body. The advantages and disadvantages of choosing the corporate format stem from this characteristic. The sole proprietorship and the general partnership are not regarded as separate entities for most legal purposes.

There are a significant number of important advantages to the corporate form of business. These can be summarized as follows:

a) The stockholder's liability is ordinarily limited to the amount of money invested in the corporate stock. The owners of the business as stockholders are not legally responsible as individuals for the debts of the business. This form of organization enables the investor to limit his risk or liability to the exact amount which he invests in the business. If the business venture should become insolvent, the creditors can look only to the corporation's assets for payment of their debts. They cannot legally request the individual stockholders to make good these corporate debts.

b) The corporation is a permanent type of organization. The death of a stockholder does not normally have a serious impact upon the business of the corporation. It may continue as long as its charter states; ordinarily, most charters of corporations are perpetual. Should a stockholder die, the stock will be transferred to the heirs and legatees of the deceased with the corporation continuing to do business as before. Similarly, if the owners or any of them should desire to sell the business, there is no necessity for terminating the business. Any stockholder, unless he has otherwise agreed with the other stockholders, may transfer his stock at any time to any other person, but the corporation will continue on exactly as it has before.

c) The principal reason for the development of the corporate method of doing business was that it offered a convenient medium for acquiring capital. The corporation is a highly desirable vehicle for pooling capital. Where large-scale operations are envisaged, and it is necessary to accumulate funds, then the corporate form of business is extremely useful since it permits the corporation to attract a great number of investors who will each purchase a percentage of its stock. This format offers great flexibility for creating types of participations in ownership. An endless variety of securities can be issued to the individuals furnishing funds, thus permitting a high degree of options for obtaining capital. Ease of transferability of ownership in the business by use of shares has appeal to the individual investor.

d) Finally, centralized management offers unity and security of control.

There are certain definite disadvantages to the operation of a business in the corporate form of organization. Ordinarily, the tax burden on corporations is higher than it is on individuals. In an individual proprietorship, or in a partnership, the owners pay a tax only on all of the profits or monies they may have gained from the business during the year. With a corporation, it pays income tax, a tax on profits and excess profits, and a tax on unreasonable surplus. Thereafter, if it distributes any of its profits to its stockholders by way of dividends, the individual stockholders will also have to pay a tax on the dividends. Thus, the monies which represent profits to the stockholders as the owners of the business are double-taxed. In the alternative, the corporate form may provide tax ad-

13

vantages if one uses profits to expand the business. Corporate tax rates are generally lower than individual rates in the higher brackets. Reinvesting earnings into the corporation can be done without the necessity of paying high individual taxes.

In addition to the regular income tax rates, there are other less significant tax burdens on a corporation, such as the organization fees, annual state franchise taxes, transfer taxes on sales of stock, etc. Clearly any businessman must consider and evaluate what the tax results of his operation through the corporate form of business are likely to before electing to use this means of doing business.

Since the corporation is created by the State through its statutes, certain very definite legal procedures are required before the organization can come into existence. This formality of organization includes initial and annual fees and taxes, drafting of incorporation documents, notices, minutes, reports and public filing requirements, which often prove prohibitive for small businesses desiring to operate freely and informally. A corporation is often required by law to have a minimum authorized, subscribed, or paid-in capital.

Essentially, the first steps in creating a corporation requires consultation with one's attorney and business associates. Preliminary thought must be given to several categories of questions:

a) Who are all the parties, names and addresses, forming the business organization;

b) what is the purpose of the business;

c) in what state will business be conducted;

d) what is the proposed structure of the business;

e) what are the anticipated earnings of the business and projected corporation tax bracket;

f) are the parties involved in other corporations together and in what percentage of ownership;

g) what is the relationship of the owners;

h) will assets other than cash be sold or conveyed by the owners;

i) what funds do the owners expect to withdraw from the business and at what times;

j) how much capital will remain in the business;

k) what is the expected operating life of the business;

l) what are the possible sources of liability;

m) how will the business affect the owner's estates;

n) is a buy and sell arrangement contemplated?

Satisfactory resolution of the above questions establishes the base on which the corporation can be created. Essentially, a Certificate (or Articles) of Incorporation is drawn up and then filed with the Secretary of State (or similar state official) of the state in which the corporation is being formed. Some states also require that a copy of the Certificate be filed with the Register of Deeds office in the county or city in which the registered office of the corporation is located. This Certificate of Incorporation is the corporation's charter, setting forth the name of the corporation and the type of business in which it may be engaged, as well as incidental matters, such as, the stock structure of the corporation, the corporation's business address, the number of directors who will be required to operate its business, etc. The internal operations of a corporation are governed by its bylaws.

Upon incorporation, the parties involved can expect to pay certain fees to the state as required by statute. These fees in most states will include:

1 - Application fee.

2 - Filing and recording fee.

3 - Capitalization fee.

4 - Fees for extra copies of articles of incorporation.

5 - Certified copy of articles fee.

6 - Certified copy of annual report fee.

7 - Filing of corporate annual report fee.

8 - Fee for corporate name change.

9 - Filing fee to change registered agent.

10 - Amendment to articles fee.

11 - Stock transfer fees.

It is thus apparent that the decision of what type of business organization to utilize is a very serious one, which can only be made intelligently after a consideration of all of the factors involved. No one form of doing business is completely perfect, giving the owners only advantages and no disadvantages. The person going into business must decide in advance what sort of advantages are most important to him, and what types of disadvantages he is willing to put up with. If the most important thing to him is a limitation on the risk involved, naturally, he will decide upon the corporate form of business.

15

If, on the other hand, he does not feel the risks will be too great, and does not wish to assume the additional cost of operation through a corporation, he may utilize an individual proprietorship or a partnership form of business. Since the problems involved are numerous, he will require expert legal guidance for his decision. In any event, he should not reach a determination until he has carefully considered all factors involved.

Close Corporation

Numerically, the vast majority of business corporations are small. Small businesses in this country employ over 30,000,000 individuals and account for some 40 percent of the total American business activity. By size of assets in 1969, those corporations with $100,000 or less in assets made up 57.6 percent of the total national corporate assets. Corporations with assets of $100,000 to $999,999 followed with 35.8 percent and firms of over $1,000,000 or more in assets were responsible for less than 6 percent of total asset accumulation.

The close corporation is sometimes referred to as the closely-held corporation. Its significance is that it is a corporation whose shares of stock are substantially held by one individual. The stockholder in such a case usually has complete and exclusive control. Another basic type of closely held corporation is that in which two or more persons or interests are represented. Here each individual has his rights preserved, but no one person has exclusive control. Voting shares of the close corporation are not issued or traded to the public as is done with the public-issue corporation.

Its shareholders are generally those individuals who are active in the conduct and management of the business. These insiders desire to keep out outsiders and require simple and informal business procedures. By acting as a corporation, the members of a closely held business receive all the advantages of being incorporated while maintaining the advantages of smallness, as found in a partnership or individual proprietorship. The close corporation is required to comply with the same statutory formalities as are required of all corporations in general. However, the problems of drafting the forms of agreement are substantially greater than those required for a normal incorporation. Special limitations and requirements demanded by the parties involved to assure proper control within the small corporation often require lengthy and detailed incorporation agreements.

Professional Corporations

It was not until the early 1960s that state statutes, ethical codes, and licensing standards began to recognize the need for professional practitioners to incorporate. Historically, the ban on professional incorporation was explained by a desire to maintain the individual and personal responsibility of the practitioner to the client, to avoid any possibility of a nonprofessional obtaining control of the licensed practioner's relationship to his client, as well as to maintain a clear line of unlimited personal liability of the professional to his client. Meanwhile, great pressure was exhibited by practitioners to obtain for themselves the advantages of pension, insurance, and other tax-sheltered benefits permitted to corporate employees and executives under the Internal Revenue Code, but denied to the partnership of sole proprietorship. By 1969 the Internal Revenue Service had recognized the right of professional groups to incorporate or associate where permitted by State Law, and to have these newly-created business entities taxed as corporations for federal revenue purposes.

At this time all the states, including the District of Columbia, have enacted some kind of statute permitting professional persons -- lawyers, doctors, dentists, certified public accountants, chiropractors, engineers, veterinarians, pharmacists, optometrists, plus many others -- to organize into professional corporations or, as defined in some states, professional associations.

The end result of these statutory provisions is the permitting of professional persons to carry on their practices in a business format that can be classified for federal income tax purposes as a corporation. Thus, these practitioners can enjoy the tax advantages offered by establishing pension and profit-sharing plans, as well as such fringe benefits as group life and health insurance plans, excludable sick pay, and death benefits. The professional may also elect to be taxed like a partnership under the tax-option corporation as defined by the Internal Revenue Code. This election might avoid corporate tax on any of the income of the corporation or the association.

Nontax-related advantages of professional corporations

17

are more practical than theoretical. Theoretically, a professional association can be created and administered with almost the identical nontax-related advantages as the corporation. The principal advantages are varied.

a) Central Control. Centralized management through an elected body expedites managerial decisions, promotes continuity and consistency in management policies, and provides an authoritative body with power to act;

b) Continuity of Existence. Continuity of life through the corporate form avoids the cessation of the enterprise that results from the death of a sole proprietor or partner. Most professional corporation laws specifically provide that if the articles of incorporation or bylaws fail to state a price or method of determining a price at which the corporation or its shareholders may purchase the shares of a deceased shareholder, or a shareholder no longer qualified to own shares, then the price of such shares will be determined by the arbitration pursuant to the rules of the American Arbitration Association. If a request for arbitration is not made in thirty days, some statutes provide that the fair value will then be determined by the district court without a jury. Thus, a specific procedure is available to allow the corporation to continue to function uninterrupted by failure of the incorporations to provide a method to determine the value of shares of stock of a deceased or disqualified professional.

c) Transferability of Interests. Most professional corporation laws make provisions for the transfer of shares of a professional corporation. Although certain restrictions may be placed on the transferability of shares, the mere fact that the shareholder's interest is represented by tangible certificates of stock representing a percentage of ownership in the corporation in and of itself provides a vehicle for the easy transfer of interest subject to the restrictions of the statute and the articles and bylaws of the corporation;

d) Limited Liability. Limited liability is available under most professional association statutes with reference to all dealing of the corporation not related to the rendering of professional services. For example, liability related to a mortgage, a lease on office space, and supplies ordered, should be restricted to the extent of corporate assets. However, liability connected with the performance of professional services licensed by the state, under many statutes often falls directly on the professional concerned. The only limited liability for professional shareholders would be available to those not directly involved in the professional service under litigation.

e) Extraordinary Transactions. A professional group may desire to join with their specialized practice the management and purchase of land and buildings. The professional corporation statutes generally permit such an opportunity to join both the professional management of a corporation with the management of the business property. Ownership, management, and operation of real property for the use of the corporation can be handled on a limited liability basis through the same set of books used for the other activities of the firm.

It appears that the proper business organization of professional groups and offices will provide an opportunity to increase efficiency by providing ways to maximize net revenue while reducing costs of professional services to the public. Reduction in employee attrition can result through the availability of incentives to capable individuals while offering advantages for attracting new and vital associates to one's professional practice.

It must be noted that each state's statute must be consulted and proper legal advice sought by those individuals interested in professional incorporation. Each statute does not necessarily use the same language nor do they fall into an identical pattern. Some statutes via their legislation permit only one professional group to incorporate, whereas other states extend the privilege to many (if not all) professions subject to licensing requirements. In addition, some states allow individual practitioners to incorporate whereas other states require a minimum of two or more professionals for the association to be lawful. Of great importance is the statutory requirements directing the future of the professional corporation should any shareholder, officer, director, or employee lose his professional license to practice. Normally, this results in the termination of the corporation or the forfeiture of the corporate character.

Chapter 2

PARTNERSHIP AND STOCKHOLDER AGREEMENTS

Once the basic form of business organization has been
settled upon, the next matter of organization to be disposed of
is the agreement between the "partners." In this connection
it is well to remember that in most small businesses where
a corporate form of organization is used, the parties involved
nevertheless in effect consider themselves as "partners,"
and seek to retain some of the attributes of a partnership
despite use of the corporate form. In this type of situation, the
corporation is called a "closed" corporation, since the management and the ownership of the business are substantially
identical. In such cases, the parties frequently will enter into
what is known as a "stockholder's agreement." This type of
agreement among stockholders in a closed corporation is, in
many respects, similar to a partnership agreement between
the members of a true partnership, though, of course, certain
differences necessarily arise because of the legal distinctions
between the two different types of organizations.

Often the persons who form partnerships or closed
corporations for the purpose of operating a small business are
either relatives or close personal friends. As a result, there
is a natural tendency on their part to avoid excessive legal
documents. While this is quite understandable, there are
important advantages to having a formal written agreement
between the partners, which will embody their understanding
with respect to the organization and operation of the business.

For one thing, the necessity of putting the matter into
writing will require the parties to reach a definite understanding on a wide variety of matters that they might not
otherwise have considered, or that would be left indefinite,
if the arrangement between them was purely oral. Further, the
legal counsel whom they consult, for the purpose of drafting
the instrument, will undoubtedly suggest to them a number of
matters that they might otherwise have overlooked. He will
also be in a position to suggest alternate ways of working out
their problems. It must also be remembered that at some
time in the future persons other than those presently involved

in the formation of the business may be interested in it. For example, in the event of the death of one of the partners, his heirs may accede to his legal interest in the business.

Experience has shown that it is extremely good foresight to have a written agreement between partners, or stockholders in a closed corporation, no matter how close their personal relationship may be. The existence of the agreement will avoid many possible future conflicts, and, in addition, will help to resolve with a minimum of difficulty those conflicts that arise. It is therefore strongly suggested that no matter how close the personal relationship between the parties may be, they enter into a formal written instrument between themselves at the outset.

While there are some necessary differences between partnership and stockholder agreements, the great majority of the provisions in such agreements will cover essentially the same matters. A simple form of a stockholders' agreement that has been used in connection with a retail drycleaning and tailoring business is provided as Appendix G and should be consulted at this point.

It will be seen that this type of agreement covers, generally, the organization and operation of the business, and has specific provisions to cover management of the business, transfer of ownership, etc. These are essentially the same types of matters that will be covered in the ordinary partnership agreement. The following matters are ordinarily included in both partnership and stockholder agreements:

Organizing the business. In the ordinary, simple partnership agreement, a statement will be made as to the name under which the parties will do business, and the address they will use for this purpose. Some general statement should also be included as to the purposes of the partnership business.

In connection with a corporation, as we have seen in Chapter 1, the name and business address will be fixed in the certificate of incorporation. So, too, the business purposes of the corporation will be set forth in that certificate. If the stockholders' agreement is signed after the parties have already formed the corporation, the reference to these matters in their agreement may be slight. On the other hand, such stockholder agreements are sometime entered into even before the corporation is formed. In that case, just as with the partnership agreement, some general statement should be made as to the name and address to be used by the corporation, and the purposes for which it is being formed.

The term of the enterprise. Ordinarily, a corporation's charter provided for continuance of the business in perpetuity. So, too, most partnerships do not have any specific limitation on the term of the partnership or corporation.

Financing the business. Both stockholder and partnership agreements will, of course, contain provisions as to the amount of capital to be contributed by the various members. In a partnership this is generally a very simple matter: there is a specific statement of the amount to be contributed by each. With a corporation, the matter is somewhat complicated by the fact that the investment is actually in the corporate shares rather than in the assets of the business itself. It will be noticed that in the form of agreement referred to above, the actual contribution of the shareholders is broken down into two separate parts, and a major portion of the contribution is actually set up as a loan to the corporation rather than by way of stock purchase. This is a device that is very frequently used in connection with closed corporations, as it enables withdrawal of profits as nontaxable loan repayments, rather than as taxable income or dividends.

The question of original investment can become exceedingly complicated when one or more of the partners contributes something other than cash. For example, it frequently happens that one of the partners contributes either a going business or some particular items of equipment or inventory. In such cases, extreme care must be exercised to insure that this contribution is fairly evaluated, and, in addition, that the new business is not saddled with any outstanding debts or liabilities unless they have been specifically taken into account in setting the value of this partner's contribution.

Profit and loss. Ordinarily, the potential profits and losses of the business are to be shared in the same proportion as the parties make their respective contributions of capital. In a partnership agreement there generally will be a specific statement of such sharing. In connection with a corporation, on the other hand, the sharing of

23

profit and loss flows directly from ownership of the corporate stock, and no specific agreement therefore has to be made with respect to it.

In most small businesses the contributions of the parties involved are equal, and they share profits and losses equally. There is no legal requirement of this sort, however. In addition, though it is not the usual situation, the parties may actually arrange to share profits and losses in some different proportion from that which would normally flow from their respective contributions of capital to the enterprise. This is frequently the arrangement where two parties form a business, and one is expected to provide the "know how" and experience, whereas the other is expected to provide the greater portion of the capital. In such situations, even though the original capital contributions are very unequal, the parties may nevertheless agree that they are to share the actual profits of the business equally.

Salaries. Generally speaking, in most small businesses, all of the parties involved are expected to work and to contribute their time to the business. Again, this is not necessarily so and frequently a "silent" partner will contribute backing for the venture but will have little to do with its day to day business operation. The agreement between the parties, whether it be a stockholder agreement or a partnership agreement, should specify the duties of each of the persons, and should also state what their relative drawings and salaries shall be.

Management of the business. On this matter, the stockholders' agreement is necessarily somewhat more complicated than the partnership agreement. The partnership agreement will ordinarily provide that the partners are to have equal rights in the management of the business; though again, there is nothing to prevent the partners from granting some of the members greater rights than those given to others, as where an old partnership is reorganized to take in new junior partners.

In connection with a corporation, specific provisions must be made with respect to the election of the officers and directors who will operate the business. See, for example, paragraphs (8) and (9) of the form of stockholders' agreement which is set out in Appendix G.

Either the stockholders' or the partnership agreement

24

may be elaborated in this connection to cover as many specific management factors as the parties wish to fix in their agreement. For instance, many such arrangements contain provisions with respect to the enterprise's bank account, the signature of checks, the signing of contracts, etc.

Termination of the business. As we have noticed in Chapter 1, one of the principal advantages of the corporate form of business is that it makes possible the continuance of the business entity even though one of the parties involved decides to sell out. At the same time, since the stockholders in a closed corporation are essentially in the nature of partners, it is clear that not one of them would want the others to sell out to a stranger. In order to avoid this, provisions are ordinarily included in stockholder agreements that restrict any of the stockholders from selling their shares to outsiders until they have been first offered for sale to the remaining stockholders. This is usually done by giving an option to the remaining shareholders to purchase the stock of a retiring partner. In this connection, the most difficult problem to be solved is the setting of the price to be paid for such shares. It is naturally impossible to determine with any degree of accuracy what the value of such shares may be in the future. Numerous methods have been evolved to settle this problem. The simplest and probably the most common provision made in stockholder agreements is that the shares be sold and purchased at their book value.

Similar provisions may likewise be incorporated into partnership agreements, so that in the event of the prospective retirement of any partner, the remaining partners will be given an option to continue the business by purchasing his share. Here, too, the problem of determing the fair purchase price for such share is an intricate and difficult one in which the advice of an attorney and accountant is highly desirable.

Closely related to this matter of the purchase of the shares of a retiring partner is the question of the effect to be given to his death or disability. In most stockholder agreements, this matter is specifically covered, and the provisions in paragraph (7) of the sample agreement (Appendix G) are fairly usual. Here, too, the remaining shareholders are given the option to purchase

25

the stock of the deceased or disabled partner, on generally somewhat the same terms as are made with respect to partnerships as they are with corporations.

Whenever the remaining shareholders or partners are given an option to purchase, it is important to provide the manner in which the purchase price will be paid. Frequently such payment is made on some form of installment basis, since very likely, where a small business is involved, the remaining partners will not have the cash available to make complete payment immediately. The use of "business" life insurance has become exceedingly popular in recent years in connection with options to purchase upon death. The idea of such insurance is to give the remaining partner sufficient capital, to be realized from the life insurance paid on the death of the deceased partner, so that he will be able to pay out the largest portion of the purchase price at once. This is a benefit to both the purchasing partner and the family of the deceased. Insofar as the purchaser is concerned, it enables him to make payment without putting an undue financial burden upon him. On the other hand, it guarantees to the deceased's family that they will realize monies from his share of the business within a reasonably short time after his death.

The form of stockholders' agreement, which is set forth in Appendix G (or a correspondingly simple form of partnership agreement), would ordinarily be sufficient to cover the usual retail or other small business. The forms can be expanded and elaborated upon to cover any variety of additional matters which the parties desire to fix and determine in their agreement, and which relates to the organization of the business and its management.

Chapter 3

THE FRANCHISED BUSINESS

An increasingly popular form of doing business is the business franchise. According to trade association statistics, in 1966 this multi-billion dollar industry was represented by well over 600,000 franchised operations in this country excluding gasoline and automobile dealerships. The franchised outlet represents all aspects of the retail business from the coin operated laundry to the fried chicken emporium.

A franchise can be defined as a license granted by the owner of a trademark or trade name permitting another to sell a service or product under that trade name or trademark. Inherent in this definition is the understanding that the owner of the trade name will fulfill his duty to the public by insuring the quality of the product or service sold under his mark or name. Thus, a franchise is primarily a device for exploiting an established trademark or trade name. The essence of any franchise system is the establishment of a quasi-independent businessman subject to various controls respecting his business operations, the nature of which depends in part on the philosophy of the franchisor and on the nature of the products and services franchised. However, some form of control over the franchisee is an essential ingredient of the franchise system.

The Federal Trade Commission has defined the elements of a franchise operation as follows:

> . . .every aspect of the relationship between a franchisor and a franchisee by an oral or written agreement or understanding, or series of agreements or understandings, or transactions which involve or result in a continuing commercial relationship by which a franchisee is granted or permitted to offer, sell, or distribute the goods or commodities manufactured, processed, or distributed by the franchisor, or the right to offer or sell services established, organized, directed, or approved by the franchisor, under circumstances where the franchisor continues to exert any control over the method of operation of the franchisee, particularly, but not exclusively, through

27

trademark, trade name, or service mark licensing, or
structural or physical layout of the franchisee's business.

See Federal Trade Commission. Proposed Rule, Disclosure Requirements and Prohibitions Concerning
Franchising, November 10, 1971.

Most franchise operations involve the sale of a product
or service to the public through one of three basic retail
business methods. First, the distributorship is that system
in which the manufacturer, as the franchisor, licenses another businessman, as franchisee, to sell his product either
exclusively, or in conjunction with other similar products.
If the franchisee is given an exclusive right to vend the product
within a specific territory this is classified as a product
franchise. Second, the chain-style business is when the franchisee operates his business under the franchisor's trade name,
follows the standardized or pre-established methods of operation,
and is generally identified as a member of a select group of
dealers. This method of operation permits the franchisor to
dictate to the franchisee such matters as size and shape of
his place of business, its location, the products to be sold,
advertising and sales methods, hours of operation, prices
charged, and others. Third, operation of a processing or manufacturing plant for making a product with established ingredients
or by a formula provided by the franchisor and in keeping with
his standards permits a franchisee to produce an item otherwise restricted.

The development of a business through an independent
franchise operation is profitable because it is predicated
upon an investment by the franchisee in his own separate
business unit and the restriction of his financial contribution
to the activities of that unit. Each unit operator, on the other
hand, creates his own franchised unit with the support of the
good will and retail attraction developed by the franchisor
through its activities and the activities of the other franchisees. Each franchisee benefits from the economics of mass
purchasing, advertising, product development, and high standards
organized by the franchisor.

For the ordinary businessman there are serious problems
involved in seeking to do business as a franchise operation.
Of major significance is the problem of the extensive controls
the franchisor seeks to impose on the business activities and
methods of its franchisees. These include standards of design

for the physical structure of the business, source of supply, and standards of quality and service. Ordinarily, a business-man has the right to do business or to refuse to do business with whomever he chooses. When one becomes a franchised operation one often finds his hours of operation, method of personnel selection, and advertising means controlled by his franchise contract. The controls established by the franchisor are ostensibly created to protect the value of the good will inherent in the franchise but often result in a substantial re-striction on the operator's business activities. For those considering investing in a franchise business the following guide-lines should be carefully evaluated.

Who is the Franchisor?

If the franchisor is well known, has a good reputation, and has an obviously successful franchising operation, you can naturally proceed with greater confidence than if little is known about him.

In either event, however, you should find out everything you can about the operation including the number of years it has been in existence, whether the franchisor has all the successful franchisees he claims to have and whether he has a reputation for honesty and fair dealing with his franchise holders. It is suggested that personal contact with his fran-chisees is an excellent way to learn about the franchisor. Therefore, obtain the names and addresses of a representative number of franchisees, travel to see them, and interview them regarding all aspects of the operation. In addition to gaining valuable information concerning the franchisor, this will un-doubtedly provide you with an opportunity to view samples of the franchise products, equipment, advertising materials, and to obtain profit data and other pertinent information reflective of the operation. Be wary of a franchisor who does not freely give you the names and addresses of his franchisees. To assure that you obtain a representative list of franchisees, ask for all franchisees operating in the particular geographical areas in which you plan to make personal contact.

The financial standing and business reputation of the franchisor would also be of utmost interest to you. In this regard sources such as Dun and Bradstreet and the Better Business Bureau should be consulted.

Occasionally, a dishonest promoter will use a franchise

name and trademark deceptively similar to that of a well known franchisor. Be certain that you are dealing with the particular franchise organization you are in fact interested in, and that the individual representing this franchise has authority to act in its behalf.

Be skeptical of franchisors whose major activity is the sale of franchises and whose profit is primarily derived from these sales or from the sale of franchise equipment. This may be the tip-off on an unscrupulous operator. In any event, it appears that such an organization would tend to exhibit far less interest or concern in the continuing success of its franchisees than what would be present in a sound franchise operation.

Remember, the more you learn about the franchisor, and his operation, before making a decision about the franchise, the less likely you will become involved in a situation that you will regret later.

The Franchise Commodity

You should determine the length of time the commodity has been marketed and whether it has been a successful promotion during this time. Is it a proven product or service, and not a gimmick?

Ask yourself whether you are genuinely interested in selling the particular product or service and whether it will have an adequate market in your territory at prices you will have to charge. Will it compare in price and performance with similar products of your potential competitors?

You should also carefully weigh future consumer demand for the commodity. Be skeptical of items which are untested in the market place or which are obviously fads. It may be helpful to you in assessing future market potential to consider whether the commodity is a staple, luxury or fad item. Generally speaking, the demand for luxury items will tend to be more uncertain than the demand for staples since demand for the former is more apt to be reflective of prevailing economic conditions.

If a product rather than a service is involved, you should be certain that it is safe, that it meets existing quality standards, and that there are no restrictions upon its use. Find out if the product is protected by patent or liability insurance and if the same protection would be afforded to you as a franchisee.

Finally, would you be compelled under the franchise agreement to sell any new products or services which may be subsequently introduced by the franchisor after you have opened the business? On the other hand, would you be permitted under the agreement to sell products and services other than the franchise commodities, if you would desire to do so at some future date?

Cost of the Franchise

In some instances, promoters in attempting to portray a franchise opportunity in its most favorable light, fail to clearly spell out the total cost of the franchise. The franchise promotion may only refer to the cash outlay that would be needed to purchase the franchise with no mention being made that it is only a down payment or that other charges and assessments may be levied incidentally to the operation of the franchise.

In assessing the total cost of the franchise, therefore, you should determine whether any balance is due over and above the down payment. How is the balance to be financed? (Interest rates would of course be a concern to you.) You should also clearly establish what is purchased with the down payment. Is it in whole or in part only a franchise fee? If so, is the franchise fee justified when considering the business reputation you will have purchased with it? Did the down payment purchase any other equity such as the building?

You will also want to know where to purchase equipment and fixtures necessary for opening the business. If these are purchased through the franchisor, are his prices comparable with competitive prices for these items on the open market?

What about supplies? Frequently franchisors will attempt to secure income on a continuing basis through the sale of supplies to their franchisees. If this is part of the proposed arrangement, how will the price of these supplies be established? What assurance do you have that the prices will be reasonable or competitive? Does the franchise agreement prohibit you from purchasing these supplies from other sources? Could you obtain identical supplies from another source at a lower price?

Another method franchisors use to charge franchisees

on a continuing basis is the assessment of royalties based upon a percentage of gross sales. Be careful that these royalties are not out of line with the sales volume and projected net profits for the franchise.

Moreover, you should not overlook the possibility that franchisors also occasionally assess franchisees an additional percentage of gross sales to cover the franchisee's share of advertising costs.

Finally, in evaluating the franchise costs in the light of your financial position, you should also consider the additional miscellaneous funds and operating capital that will be needed to get the business underway and to sustain it during the early weeks and months when profits will undoubtedly be small and expenses unusually high.

What Profits Can Reasonably Be Expected?

There is no question that many franchise arrangements provide excellent income-producing opportunities. It would be ridiculous to assume, however, that all franchises yield the fantastic profits sometimes promised in franchise promotions or documented in human interest stories about franchising. They do not, and in fact many of them produce profits far less than those represented by franchise promoters. Indeed, when purely deceptive promotions are involved, debts rather than fantastic profits are generated.

Since anticipated profits are frequently the overriding motivation for entering a franchise business, promoter representations concerning earning potential or projected net profits should not be taken for granted. You should scrutinize these representations carefully, verify them for accuracy, and satisfy yourself that the figures presented are realistic and can in fact be attained by you. Ask to see certified profit figures of franchisees operating on a level of activity you can reasonably expect. You will, of course, in your personal contacts with franchisees, quiz them regarding the financial rewards they have experienced through their respective enterprises. Always remember to evaluate the profit figures and comments of these individuals in the light of the territory and size of operation you have under consideration.

What Training and Management Assistance Will Be Provided By the Franchisor?

Most franchisors purport to train their franchisees. The type and extent of training varies broadly, however, from perhaps one day's indoctrination on the one hand to a more lengthy meaningful training program on the other. Naturally, when the franchisor provides good training opportunities, the franchisee enjoys brighter prospects for survival and prosperity. Such training will tend to enable him to cope with the specific tasks he must perform in the business.

Frequently, franchise promoters use representations such as "no prior experience necessary." In some instances, however, contrary to the falsely reassuring representations of the promoter, the training provided is inadequate and fails to overcome the inexperience of the franchisee. These circumstances produce unhappy and disappointing results.

It is very important, therefore, that you clearly understand the specific nature of the training that will be provided before making a decision about the franchise. Will the training be more extensive than receiving a manual of instructions or hearing a few lectures? What is the length of the training and where must you go to receive it? Who will pay your expenses during the training period? Will the training include an opportunity to observe and perhaps work with a successful franchisee for a meaningful period of time? Do you honestly feel that after taking the training offered you will be capable of operating this franchise successfully?

Continuing management assistance after the business has been established may also be promised by the franchisor. The nature of this assistance is occasionally specified in the franchise agreement, but more often than not only a broad general commitment is included. When being specific, the franchisor may promise to assist with a management or employee training program, an advertising program, merchandising ideas, or in any number of other ways. Here too, it is important to find out precisely the nature of the assistance you can expect to receive and its cost to you.

For example, if advertising aid is promised, will it be in the form of handbills, brochures, signs, radio or newspaper advertising? If you would be required to participate in a franchisor-sponsored promotion program by contributing a percentage of your profits to an advertising fund, what specific advertising benefits can you anticipate and at what dollar cost?

Some franchisors represent that their franchisees will receive management assistance through periodic visits to the business establishment of the franchisee by supervisory personnel of the franchisor. You should find out the specific nature of the assistance offered during these visits and the frequency with which they occur. What assurance do you have that such personnel will be available for consultation in times of crisis or when unusual problems arise?

The Franchise Territory

The franchise territory is a critical factor to consider in evaluating a prospective venture. Following are some questions that may help you to assess this aspect of the franchise. What specific territory is being offered? Is it clearly defined? What is its potential? Do you have a choice of territories? What competition would you meet in marketing the commodity in the designated territory today? How about five years from now? Has the franchisor represented that a market survey has been made of the proposed territory? If so, who prepared it? Ask him for a copy of it and read it carefully. What assurance do you have that the territory you select is an exclusive territory? In other words, would you be protected from the possibility of the franchisor selling additional franchises within the territory at a later date? On the other hand, are there any limitations upon you in the event you desire to open additional outlets in the territory, or even another territory, at some future time? Has the specific business site within the territory been selected? If not, how will this be decided?

Termination, Transfer and Renewal

Inasmuch as oppressive termination provisions can cause unexpected and sometimes severe financial loss to a franchisee, careful consideration should be given to this aspect of the agreement.

As an example, some franchise agreements provide that at the end of the contract term, or during the contract term if in the opinion of the franchisor certain conditions have not been met, the franchisor has the absolute right to terminate the agreement. The contract generally provides the franchisor with an option to repurchase the franchise if he so desires. If the franchisor should terminate the agreement under these circumstances and if the contract does not provide a means whereby a fair market price for the franchise can be established, it may be possible for the franchisor to repurchase the business at an arbitrarily low and unfair price.

On occasion, franchisors have gone so far as to include a provision in the agreement to the effect that the repurchase price should not exceed the original franchise fee. This means that after a franchisee may have expended considerable effort and funds building the business into a profitable enterprise, he may be faced with the unhappy prospect of having to sell it back to the franchisor at a price no greater than he paid for it years earlier. Under such an obviously unfair provision, the franchisee would not be compensated for the good will or increased equity which he contributed to the business.

Thus, it is important that you, as a prospective franchisee, are aware of the conditions under which the agreement could be terminated and that you clearly understand your rights in the event of termination. You should determine whether the contract extends to the franchisor the right of cancellation for almost any reason or must there be good cause? Beware of contracts that under the threat of cancellation impose unreasonable obligations such as, a minimum monthly purchase of goods, or services from the franchisor or unrealistic sales quotas. How would the value of the franchise be determined in the event of termination? Under what circumstances could you terminate the agreement and at what cost to you? Does the contract contain a restrictive covenant that would prohibit you from engaging in a competitive business in the franchise territory in the event termination occurs?

It is equally important that you have a clear understanding of any contract provisions dealing with your ability to transfer or renew the franchise. What restrictions would there be in the event you desired to transfer or sell the franchise? What would happen to the franchise in the event of your death? Under what circumstances would you be able to renew the franchise agreement at the end of the contract term?

Remember, a good franchise opportunity will permit a franchisee to own and build an equity interest in his franchise, which he, in turn, can sell for whatever value the franchise may have realized under his direction. Some reputable franchisors who have established fair and permanent relationships with their franchisees have made provision for an arbitration clause which allows for a fair evaluation of the franchisee's contribution in the event of termination. In this manner the franchisee will not only recoup his initial investment but will also realize a profit on the sale of whatever good will he may have generated in the business.

Is the Franchise Attractive Because It Carries the Name of a Well-Known Personality?

Some concern has recently been expressed to the effect that franchising may be bursting at the seams with name personalities. This is not to suggest that franchises identified with personalities are unworthy of consideration. The important thing to keep in mind is the degree of participation the personality brings to the business. Is he just a figurehead with no actual capital investment of his own in the enterprise? Will he make substantial personal contributions of time and effort to promote the venture to the mutual benefit of all franchisees in the organization? What assurance do you have that he will make personal appearances at your business if such have been promised? Does this personality have a name of lasting value in identifying your franchise to the consuming public? How sound is the basic franchise operation when viewed apart from the prominent name?

Is the Promoter Primarily Interested In Selling Distributorships?

Be wary of promoters who are primarily interested in selling distributorships, probably for some new wonder product. Exaggerated income promises are common in these promotions. Generally, according to the promotional plan, the distributor is to recruit subdistributors or salesmen who are supposed to sell the product, usually by door-to-door sales. Theoretically, a large portion of the distributor's profits are to be derived from a percentage of his subdistributor's sales. Unfortunately, however, distributors and the subdistributors he successfully recruits frequently find, to their mutual distress, after making sizable investments of money, time, and effort, that they reap little profit and are stuck with a large stock of a virtually unsalable product.

Is It a Route Servicing Promotion?

Be alert for deceptive route servicing promotions. Typically, promotions of this kind are characterized by misleading representations (frequently appearing in newspaper want ads) concerning exaggerated profits and the availability of quality routes. If equipment, such as vending machines, is to be purchased in connection with the promotion, it may be poorly made and highly priced. Compare the equipment and prices with those of reputable manufacturers. Carefully check out the validity of all statements made in these promotions, and remember, promoter promises of assistance in locating quality routes after the contract is signed are usually unfulfilled.

How About Your Qualification As A Franchisee?

Before entering into any franchise agreement you should be mindful of your personal qualifications to be a franchisee in the business you have under consideration. Ask yourself whether you are genuinely enthusiastic over the franchise plan, whether you have the ability, and whether you are physically and emotionally equipped for the work that will be necessary to develop a successful enterprise. While some franchise promoters would have you believe that through a minimum or part-time effort, or even absentee ownership, you can become extremely successful in the franchising world, experience has proven otherwise. By and large, franchisees can only expect to succeed by hard work and full-time effort. Franchise plans based on part-time work generally produce only modest results for the franchisee.

If you feel you have these qualifications, ask yourself whether you are temperamentally suited to spend your business life working with this franchisor and selling this particular product or service to the public. It may be well to remember that even though you may own your own business, as a franchisee you will necessarily sacrifice a certain degree of independence and public recognition that you may otherwise possess as a completely independent businessman. If this thought does not appeal to you, perhaps you would be better off outside franchising.

In Summary, What Steps Can You Take To Protect Yourself As A Prospective Franchisee?

a) Don't be rushed into signing a contract or any other documents relating to a franchise promotion. Be wary of pressure for an immediate contract closing for the alleged purpose of precluding others who are supposedly waiting to take the territory if you delay. Don't make any deposits or down payments to hold a franchise open, or to demonstrate good faith, or for any other reason, unless you are absolutely certain about your decision to go ahead with the franchise arrangement. Remember, reputable firms do not engage in high pressure sales tactics.

b) Find out all you can about the franchise. View the franchise proposal in the light of these guidelines and resolve all areas of uncertainty before making a decision. Ask the franchisor for some names and addresses of his franchisees. No reputable franchisor will object to giving you this information. Personally contact a representative number of these franchisees, and discuss all aspects of the operation. Have they realized all the promises made to them by the franchisor? Has the franchisor met his contractural obligations?

c) Call your local Better Business Bureau. Ask for a business responsibility report on the franchisor-promoter. The Bureau's report may help you determine whether the promoter is legitimate and whether complaints have been received from others. If your local Better Business Bureau has no information on the franchisor, contact the National Better Business Bureau, 230 Park Avenue, New York, New York, 10017.

d) Be certain that all terms of the agreement are set forth in a written contract that is not oppressive in its requirements upon you, or unfairly weighted in the favor of the franchisor.

e) Consult a lawyer and have him review all aspects of the agreement before you sign the contract, or any papers relating to the franchise. This may turn out to be the soundest investment you could have made.

f) If you have a complaint about a deceptive franchising practice, contact your local or state consumer protection agency and the Federal Trade Commission. While the Commission cannot personally assist one in recouping losses that may have been suffered, it will be able to prevent other prospective franchisees from being deceived in the same manner.

Many states have enacted laws relating to franchising, franchise contract terms, and the use of franchise offerings as securities. Many states also have laws that protect the dealer from unfair termination or from arbitrary actions of franchisors. A state by state listing of laws regulating franchising as January, 1973 appears in Appendix D . Those states not listed had no relevant statutes at the time. Some of these laws apply to specialized businesses, such as automobile dealerships, and farm equipment dealers, while others apply only to franchise offers, or only to franchise terminations. Consult your attorney to be sure of the scope of the franchise statutes in your state.

Chapter 4

PURCHASE AND SALE OF A BUSINESS

A person entering into business has the choice of either starting a new enterprise himself or of purchasing an already established business. One starting a completely new business faces many uncertainties. He does not know, for example, what gross business he is likely to do, what his cost of operation will be, or whether or not he has selected a good location. Many of these uncertainties can be either eliminated or sharply restricted by the purchase of an established enterprise. Thus, an examination of the books and records of a good retail store should tell the prospective purchaser with a reasonable degree of definiteness what amount of gross business he can expect to do at that location, and at least in a general way, what expenses he will have to face. For these reasons, many persons prefer to purchase a going business rather than to establish a new one.

The purchase of an established business, if it is at all a successful one, requires the payment of some premium over and above the actual value of its physical assets. The purchaser must determine whether the price he is asked to pay is fair and reasonable, taking into consideration the prospective profit that he may anticipate from his own operation of the business. Since no two persons will conduct a business in exactly the same manner, the profit which the purchaser can anticipate is to some degree a matter of speculation. Much of the uncertainty, however, can be eliminated by a careful study of the old business and of its books and records.

To a large extent the contract for the purchase and sale of a going business must be tailored to the specific requirements of the transaction, and there is no routine form which can be uniformly followed in all such dealings. There are, obviously, a number of important factors which should generally be taken into consideration in agreements for purchase and sale of a business. The first question to be settled is the amount of the purchase price, and the manner in which that price will be paid. Ordinarily, a portion of the purchase price will be paid upon the execution of the original contract of sale. In the simplest form of transaction, the balance will be paid in cash or by certified check at the time of the actual closing of the transaction. Frequently, however, the purchaser will be unable or unwilling to make full cash payment outright. Arrangements have to be made in such situations for payment of the balance in installments, and for the purchaser to give sufficient security, insuring the seller that he will receive all of the monies he is entitled to. Often the purchaser will give his own promissory notes for this purpose. In addition, further security may be given by assigning to the seller certain accounts receivable of the business, or by placing a chattel mortgage in favor of the seller on some or all of the equipment and fixtures of the business.

The purchase price must ordinarily be adjusted at the time of closing to take into consideration any items of business expenses which have been prepaid by the seller. For example, if the transfer takes place during the middle of a month, an adjustment must be made in favor of the seller to cover the rent for the full month which he has prepaid to the landlord. So, too, prepaid insurance premiums, deposits with utility companies, and any other items of business expense that have been prepaid by the seller should be taken into consideration at the time of closing. Of course, the deal may be that the purchaser will get the benefit of all such prepayments. But if that is not the arrangement between the parties, then appropriate adjustments must be made to cover such prepaid monies.

Closely related to the question of the purchase price is the matter of exactly what is being covered by the sale. This may, and will vary considerably from deal to deal. Most frequently the purchase covers the entire business as an operating concern, including all its fixtures and equipment, accounts receivable, trade name, good will, etc. However, there is no legal requirement that the transaction cover all these things. What the purchaser will actually get will depend upon the arrangements worked out between the parties, in other words, the terms of the contract control.

In this connection, the purchaser must know not only what he is going to get, but what condition the items will be in, and to what encumbrances, if any, they may be subjected. Thus, the purchaser will want to ascertain in advance whether the equipment is owned free and clear by the seller, or whether

41

it may be subject to an outstanding chattel mortgage or conditional sales agreement.

Of extreme importance is the question of the outstanding debts and liabilities of the seller. The agreement may provide that the purchaser is to take over only the assets of the business, and that the seller will remain completely responsible for all debts and liabilities. On the other hand, it is sometimes agreed that the purchaser will take the business subject to all outstanding liabilities. In such a case, the amount of such outstanding liabilities must be taken into consideration when the purchase price is fixed. In any case, it is absolutely necessary that the purchaser know exactly what the outstanding liabilities of the seller are.

In this connection attention must be paid to what is commonly known as the Bulk Sales Act. Statutes of this sort have been enacted in all states except Louisiana as part of the Uniform Commercial Code. They provide generally that when a sale of the assets of a business is made in bulk, certain formalities must be met. Ordinarily, the seller is required to give to the purchaser an affidavit setting out all of the creditors of his business, and written notice is thereafter given to the creditors before the deal is actually consummated. The purpose of these provisions is to put the creditors of the seller on notice that the sale is being made. If the formal statutory requirements are not met, the purchaser takes the equipment transferred to him subject to the claims of the seller's creditors.

A variety of devices has been employed in agreements of this sort to avoid the necessity of complying with the statutory requirements of the Bulk Sales Act. The simplest is to have the seller actually pay all of his obligations, either on or before the closing date, and then to give the purchaser an affidavit stating that he has no creditors. Since, however, the seller may not have sufficient cash on hand, or may not desire to prepay all outstanding debts, arrangement may be worked out for him to deliver to the purchaser a list of the outstanding creditors, and then to deposit in escrow a sum of money (usually deducted from the purchase price) sufficient to pay off all of these creditors in full. Sometimes the seller will balk at depositing monies in escrow and will offer instead an indemnification agreement to the purchaser, guaranteeing that all his outstanding debts will be paid. This latter form of arrangement is risky, however, from the purchaser's point of view, unless he is absolutely certain of the financial responsibility of the seller.

In any case, whatever arrangements are worked out, there should be careful audit of the seller's books, and in addition, the contract should contain a representation and warranty from the seller as to the outstanding debts of his business, and his agreement to hold the purchaser harmless with respect to them.

In certain types of business such as, personal service businesses, and professional practices, the good will and trade name of the seller are more important assets to the purchaser than the actual physical properties that are being transferred. In this connection, a restrictive covenant upon the seller's activities is of great importance. Such a restrictive covenant should be obtained in any situation in which the purchaser's business can be sharply affected by future competition from the seller. Ordinarily, a restrictive covenant will provide that the seller shall not engage in the same business or enterprise for a specified period of time within a certain fixed area.

The occupancy of the premises that has been used by the seller is ordinarily, also, a matter of primary importance to the purchaser. The seller's lease must be closely examined to make sure that he is permitted to assign or sublet to the purchaser. If he is not, then arrangements must first be made directly with the landlord to insure that the purchaser will be permitted to occupy the premises. So, too, if a state or local license is required for the operation of the business, it is pertinent to make sure that this license can be transferred to the purchaser. Thus, in connection with the sale of a restaurant which sells liquor, the approval of the State Liquor Authority must be obtained to the transfer of the certificate. Therefore, arrangements should be made in the contract of sale for application for such transfer, and the contract should be conditioned upon the obtaining of the necessary approval.

The provisions, which we have referred to above, would apply generally to any transfer. It should be noted, however, that where a corporate seller is involved, special problems may arise. In cases of sales by closed corporations, it is quite common to require that the individual stockholders of the selling corporation guarantee the contract and its provisions. Further, the deal may be arranged so that instead of a sale of the corporation's assets, the transaction may actually involve the sale of the stock of the corporation. In

43

such case, of course, the purchasers will find that they take subject to all outstanding liabilities of the selling corporation. For this reason it is not ordinarily desirable to purchase the stock of a closed corporation.

While these are the most usual matters that are covered in agreements for the purchase and sale of a business, they are by no means the only ones. The contract can and should be expanded to cover any and all other matters that have been agreed upon by the parties.

Chapter 5

NAMING THE BUSINESS

Ordinarily, a person assumes that he can select practically any name he chooses for his business enterprise. Actually, however, there are numerous legal restrictions upon the names that can be used, and various formalities must be taken into consideration whenever a business NAME is adopted.

In the simplest sort of situation -- that of an individual owner who does business under his own name -- there is ordinarily no restriction. Generally, anyone is completely free to use his own name in connection with his business without any limitation whatsoever. It occasionally happens, however, that the use of a person's own name will, either intentionally or otherwise, cause confusion. For example, let us suppose that a man named Eastman Kodak decided he wanted to go into the camera and film business. Clearly, if he called his company the Eastman Kodak Camera Company, many persons would be likely to be deceived into thinking that he had some connection with the nationally famous Eastman Kodak Company. In a situation of this sort, the court would undoubtedly put some restrictions upon the use of his own name, either by requiring him to state clearly that he had no connection with the other company, or possibly, even forbidding completely the use of his name as part of his company's business title. This, however, is the unusual situation and ordinarily any man is free to use his own name in any way he chooses in connection with his business.

If the individual proprietor uses some form of assumed or trade name for his business, there are additional restrictions upon him. For example, if John Jones decided to do business as the Excelsior Mattress Company, in most states he would be required to file a certificate with the county clerk (or similar official), setting forth the pertinent information as to ownership of business. The purpose of this type of certificate is to permit anyone who does business with the Excelsior Mattress Company to ascertain from the official records exactly who it is who owns the company.

45

A person using an assumed business name will generally be prevented by a court from adopting any name that is likely to be confusing to the public. What will be confusing is a question of fact depending upon all of the circumstances. Thus, if John Jones decides to use the name Excelsior Mattress Company and sets up in business at 1107 Broadway, clearly, confusion would be likely to result if there is already another Excelsior Matrress Company in business located across the street from him. The company which originally used this name would undoubtedly have a right to go to court and ask that its name be protected, and that the second user be prevented from using the assumed name.

On the other hand, if there was no other Excelsior Mattress Company in the same town, but there was another Excelsior Mattress Company in a town 200 miles away, it would ordinarily have no right to prevent John Jones from using the same name in his own town. If the business were not local, but actually operated in the same territory, so that persons dealing with them might be deceived or confused, then the first user might be able to prevent Jones from using the same business name, even though the home offices were in different towns. If, on the other hand, there was no competition between the two businesses, no one would be likely to be deceived and therefore Jones would not ordinarily be restricted from using the same name.

The foregoing discussion is, in simplified form, a statement of what is known as the law of unfair competition or of trade names. Essentially, the theory is that business men should compete fairly and that it is unfair for a person to adopt a name which has previously been used by another if under the circumstances his adoption of this trade name is likely to cause confusion.

The same theory applies in any sort of use of a trade name. Similar principles would apply if the trade name were adopted by a partnership rather than by John Jones, individually. Just as an individual proprietor is required to file a form with the county clerk when he adopts an assumed name, so too, partners are required to file similar certificates with the county clerk, setting forth the name of the partnership, and the individual names of all persons who are members of the partnership.

When a corporation is formed, permission to use the

46

name which is adopted must be obtained from the state official who files the certificate of incorporation. One of the paragraphs of the certificate or charter sets forth the specific name which may be used. The state keeps a record of all names adopted for corporations, and will not permit a new corporation to be formed that will use the same or very similar corporate name as that which has previously been adopted by another corporation.

In addition to the actual name that is used by the business organization as its title, the owners of the business may want to use insignia or names to designate their particular products. The latter, which are generally called trade-marks, may differ considerably from the name that is used as the company title. For example, ''Wheaties'' is actually a trade-mark used by General Mills, Inc., as the trade-mark for one of its many products. That same corporation has many, many products, for which it uses various trademarks. Essentially then, the difference between a trade-mark and a trade name is that the trade-mark is the name that is applied to a particular product or service of the business, while the trade name or assumed name is actually the name under which the business operates.

Trade-marks frequently are registered. Legally, a trade-mark is just as valid whether or not it is registered. The effect of registration is not to make the trade-mark valid, but it does give certain distinct advantages when actions are brought. The federal laws provide for the registration with the United States Patent Office of trade-marks that are used in interstate commerce, that is, commerce between two states. When a label carries the notation ''Reg. U.S. Pat. Off.,'' or ⓡ ,'' that means the trade-mark has been federally registered. A trade-mark cannot be registered with the federal government if it is only used locally. Application for same must be accompanied by a drawing depicting the trade name together with five samples or specimens of the mark as actually applied to the goods in question.

While most states have provisions for local registration of trade-marks, as a practical matter state registration of trade-marks is not of very great importance, and most firms which only use trade-marks locally do not bother to register.

Just as with trade names, the use of a similar trade-mark by another party may be restricted by the first user if the use appears to be unfair. Again, this is largely a question

47

of fact. Surely, if anyone adopted the name "Koka Kola" for a soft drink, it would be clear that that mark would be confusing with "Coca Cola," and a court would restrain this use. On the other hand, the courts have held that it is not confusing for other companies to use names such as "Dixi Cola," and "Royal Crown Cola." With respect to these latter marks, the courts have held that there is sufficient distinction between the marks and "Coca Cola" so that the ordinary purchaser would not be confused by them.

In selecting a trade-mark, therefore, care should be used to choose one which will not be likely to cause confusion with a trade-mark that has already been adopted by someone else. Naturally, it is impossible to know every mark that has ever been adopted, since many of them are unregistered, and even though they may be widely used, you may not have heard of them. One precaution which can always be taken, however, is to have a search made of the registered trade-marks that have been registered for the same type of product in the United States Patent Office. That search will at least reveal whether the mark has been previously adopted by another company doing business widely enough to feel it worth its while to register the mark. In addition to having such a search made, it is wise to try to find out through the sources in the trade, such as trade publications, whether any mark of the same sort is being used by anyone else. In the case of a strictly local business, examination of the telephone book for possibly conflicting names is important.

These are extremely technical matters, and any business man who is seriously contemplating the use of a trade name, or of a trade-mark (whether or not he intends to register it), should consult with his legal advisers before he proceeds to adopt it. Otherwise he may find that he invested his money in advertising, labels, etc., on a name or mark that he has no right to use, and that he will have to give up if he wishes to avoid legal difficulties.

Chapter 6

THE BUSINESS LEASE

It is exceedingly rare for a person starting out in business not to rent the space that he intends to occupy. There are many reasons for renting rather than purchasing property. For one thing, a purchase generally uses up a large amount of the available capital of the business, and it is usually undesirable to tie up capital in this fashion. In addition, it is very difficult in most instances to determine in advance, just how much space and what type of space will be ultimately required by the business. As a result, it is ordinarily the wiser policy in a situation of this sort to rent rather than to buy.

Despite the importance of the lease, it is the unusual business man who really knows what his lease contains. Most persons seem to feel that so long as the rent is paid, everything will be all right, and that there really is no point in bothering about the fine print of the lease. This assumption can prove to be very dangerous. The fact is that there are a great number of provisions in the lease which may, in the long run, be even more important to the tenant than the basic provisions about the amount of rent he must pay and the length of the lease.

It must be remembered that most leases are on printed forms that have been prepared ahead of time. These forms are for the most part drawn in favor of the landlord rather than the tenant. The tenant may find upon examination of the lease that, even though the rent provisions are completely satisfactory to him, there are numerous other provisions in the agreement that are very disadvantageous and would be a handicap to him. In addition, leases are drawn in technical legal language and are frequently not completely clear in their terms to one who is not an expert. For this reason, the lease should be carefully examined by the tenant's attorney. If necessary or desirable, he can attempt to have some adjustment made with respect to some of its provisions.

Of course, whether or not satisfactory adjustments in the terms of the lease can be made before it is signed will depend upon the particular situation involved. If the property is extremely desirable, and there are numerous persons who want to rent it, the landlord will not likely grant concessions or changes in the lease. On the other hand, if the landlord has trouble renting the property, or if he is getting a very good rental in the lease, he may be willing to bargain with the tenant in order to change or modify some of the unfavorable provisions in the lease. Like every other contract -- and it must be remembered that a lease is a contract -- this is a matter for bargaining and negotiation. Before the tenant can bargain or negotiate intelligently, he must know what is in the contract submitted to him.

The lease is ordinarily a lengthy and complicated document. The following is a description of some of the more important provisions which may be found in it. Many of these will not be of interest to a particular tenant. Others may be extremely pertinent. Each tenant must determine which provisions are most important to him, and then seek to obtain a lease which is as favorable as possible to himself in these regards.

Obviously, the basic provision to be considered first is the amount of rent that will have to be paid.

Ordinarily, the rental will be fixed in the lease as a flat sum per year, payments made per month. The landlord may attempt to include what is called a graduated rent, that is to say, the rent will increase from year to year or at different years during the term of the lease. For example, the rent on a five-year lease may be fixed at $100 per month for the first year, $110 per month for the next three years, and $125 per month for the last year of the lease. The tenant must be careful before signing such a lease to be sure that he can reasonably expect to meet the rent, not only in the first year of the lease, but subsequently thereafter when it is to be increased.

In addition, many landlords seek so-called percentage leases. These are particularly common in leases for retail stores. Percentage leases are of varying sorts. Most frequently, they will provide for a minimum amount per month that the landlord is satisfied to receive, with an additional provision that if the tenant does more than a certain amount of business, he must pay an increased rent based upon a percentage of such excess. Thus, a lease may provide for a minimum rent of $150 per month against 9 percent of the annual gross receipts of the business. Such leases may be fair and even desirable to the tenant, when the figures are reasonable. What may be a fair percentage for one type of business will

50

be completely unrealistic for another. This will vary, depending not only on the type of business involved, but also on the size of the town, whether the property is centrally located, and on many similar factors. The United States Department of Commerce has estimated the average percentage rents that various types of retail business may reasonably expect to pay. For example, it is estimated that liquor stores may pay between 6 and 8 percent of their income as rent, whereas shoe repair shops can pay as high as 15 to 20 percent. Obviously, the tenant must be sure of the facts of his own situation, before he can make an intelligent decision on a percentage lease. It is generally possible to ascertain, either through brokers or attorneys in a particular town, what a fair percentage lease is for a particular type of business in a certain locality.

After the rent has been fixed, a basic factor is the length or term of the lease. In this connection, there may be conflicting interests. For example, a tenant occupying a new store will not want to tie himself up for too many years, since he may very well find out that he was optimistic in his original estimates and cannot make a go of the business. On the other hand, he will want a lease that will give him a reasonably long and secure tenancy, so that if his business is successful, he will not find that he has to move after a short period of time, or to pay a greatly increased rent. Generally speaking, particularly today when in many cities good rental properties are exceedingly hard to get, it is desirable for the tenant to take a fairly long lease, except in connection with businesses which are extremely risky in their nature.

One possible variation, which can be of benefit to the tenant and still not leave him subject to a penalty on a long lease, is a lease for a relatively short period of time, with provisions permitting renewal at the option of the tenant, either on the same rental basis, or at a moderately increased rent. These renewal provisions are extremely important. They are a protection to the tenant to insure his ability to remain on the premises at the place where he established his business, without being subject to a sharp increase in rent if his lease expires.

It is important to note in the lease whether the tenant is required to pay any additional sums over and above the fixed rent. For example, in some leases the tenant is required to pay water, real estate, or other taxes. This all

51

ties in with the general question of what exactly the tenant is to receive for his rent. Does he receive gas and electric? Does he receive any special services such as, elevator services, etc.? Since these so-called fringe items can amount in total to a sizable sum, it is necessary that the tenant know just what his lease is going to give him. It is not good business to sign a lease with a low rental, and then to find later that in practical effect the rent will be sharply increased by the fact that the lease requires the tenant to bear numerous additional expenses, which he had not thought about at the time he signed the lease.

In connection with such additional expenses, the lease may provide that the tenant must take out certain types of insurance for the benefit of the landlord. For example, many leases provide for fire insurance, or in connection with retail stores, for plate glass insurance on the windows of the store. In addition, some landlords require that the tenant take out public liability insurance for the benefit of the landlord. Again, such provisions may sharply increase the amount that the tenant is actually being required to pay for the premises. This should be taken into consideration ahead of time, when the tenant is determining what the lease on the property is actually going to cost him.

Another provision that will radically affect the actual cost of the premises to the tenant is that which governs the repairs and renovations to the property. Does the lease provide, for example, that the landlord must paint, or is that an expense which the tenant will bear? Does the lease provide that the landlord will make necessary renovations in the premises in order to make them suitable for the tenant's occupancy? Sometimes a landlord -- particularly if he is having trouble in renting the premises -- will be willing to undertake the expense of extensive renovations for a desirable tenant who is willing to take a long lease. Further, who has the responsibility for bearing the cost of repairs to the premises? Frequently this responsibility is divided, it being provided that the landlord must bear the expense of all repairs to the exterior of the premises, and that the tenant will bear the expense of making any necessary repairs to the interior. This type of provision is usually found hidden, in small print, in one of the paragraphs of the lease. It may actually provide (although the tenant who has not read the lease does not realize it) that the tenant bears all repair expenses. Then, after a storm, act of God, or unforseen calamity, he may find, much to his surprise and regret, that he is completely responsible to make all repairs on the premises. Make sure then that you know just what your potential liability is in case of damage.

Another important matter is the use which the tenant may make of the premises. It is important to insure that the lease is broad enough to cover all purposes that the tenant may desire to use the property for, even taking into consideration possible future uses that are not intended at the particular moment the lease is signed.

Along the same lines, the tenant should attempt, if possible, to obtain so-called restrictive covenant provisions from the landlord. This, of course, can apply only where the landlord owns more than one store or piece of property in the immediate vicinity. Particularly with retail establishments, if the tenant is renting one store in a large group of stores owned by the same landlord, he will not ordinarily want the landlord to rent another store in the immediate vicinity for the same purpose. For example, a person renting a corner property to be used as a drug store, will not be very likely to want the landlord to rent the adjacent store to another tenant for another drug store. If the landlord is agreeable, a provision may be inserted in the lease restricting his right to lease another store in the vicinity for the same purpose.

Examine the lease to see if it permits possible assignment or subleasing of the premises. Landlords do not ordinarily like to give their tenants the right to assign or sublet the premises. On the other hand, from the tenant's point of view, this may be an extremely important provision. He may find that the premises are completely unsuitable to himself, and therefore they are burdensome to him if he is required to continue to occupy them. They may, however, be desirable for some other tenant. If he has the right to assign or sub-let, he can relieve himself of the undesirable leases. Therefore, if it is at all possible, the tenant should insist upon the right to assign or sub-let any lease, except a lease for a very short period of time. Sometimes a compromise can be worked out with the landlord, to the effect that the tenant is given such right subject only to the landlord's reasonable approval of the proposed sub-tenant.

In most modern leases, security of some sort is required from a commercial or business tenant. If the amount of security required is very great it will cut down on the capital available to the tenant for his business purposes. It is therefore important to attempt to limit the amount of security to some reasonable sum.

There are many additional matters to be found in the ordinary lease which may be important to the tenant. For example, one will want to ascertain what the tenant's rights are in case of disagreement with the landlord. What restrictions exist on the type of signs which can be used in connection with a retail store?

Clearly, there are numerous provisions in the leases that the tenant should be aware of before he signs the lease, other than the obvious ones of length of term of the lease and amount of rent. These and all similar problems should be discussed with the attorney for the tenant, so that he is fully aware of just what provisions affect his tenancy, since, in practical effect, these additional provisions may have a great bearing on the true cost of the premises to the tenant and his rights in occupying them. They should be carefully investigated before a lease is signed.

Chapter 7

THE SMALL BUSINESS ADMINISTRATION

During World War II, in 1942, the Small War Plants Corporation (SWPC) was devised as a temporary federal agency to mobilize aggressively the production capacity of all small business concerns, and to determine the means by which such concerns can be most efficiently utilized to augment war production. The Agency's primary work was to match up small companies for subcontracts with large companies and government agencies. It also did a limited amount of lending to small business, being authorized to make loans directly, or in cooperation with lending institutions, to small concerns for war or essential civilian purposes. At war's end, most of the procurement and lending authority of SWPC was transferred to the Reconstruction Finance Corporation (RFC), the giant agency created in 1932 to pull the country out of the Depression by extending credit to banks and other financial institutions. In World War II, its role was expanded to financing and building defense plants and stockpiling strategic war materials.

A specific small business aspect of RFC's work, however, did not come into being until 1948 when the Congress added the words ''to encourage small business'' to its objectives. A new war in 1950 called for new small business measures. A Senate account reported that ''. . .using the SWPC as a guide, the members of the Senate and the House Small Business Committees pressed for a similar organization during Korea. . .''

This resulted in the Small Defense Plants Administration (SDPA) in 1951 as an emergency agency with primary responsibility to channel defense contracts to small producers. Its lending authority was limited to recommending firms to the RFC. In a final report, that agency observed: ''SDPA may be considered in many ways as a pioneer in this field. It took up the reins following a five-year lapse in independent representation for small business and proved once more that opportunity for small business is best preserved by centralization of effort in a single agency. Perhaps SDPA's most notable achievement is the strength it gave to the belief. . .

that small business needs and deserves adequate representa-tion in peacetime as well as in times of national emer-gency. . . ."

With SDPA phasing out, the Congress was reluctant to let the idea die. The Senate Select Committee on Small Business said: "By the middle of 1953, it became apparent that. . . the American economy was resuming a more 'normal' chara-cter. Nonetheless, many unsolved problems remained to plague the most resourceful small entrepreneur, and Congress was convinced that it would be a mistake to scrap the mechanism developed to meet emergency crises when many substantial obstacles still strewed the path of smaller concerns merely because of their size. . ."

The Chairman of the House Select Committee on Small Business said, "Small business should be viewed not as a war-born stepchild but in its true perspective as the economic backbone of the Nation. In times of war, in times of peace, in good times and bad times. . ." The Senate Banking and Currency Committee concluded: "While in this, as in other fields, primary reliance should be placed upon individual initiative and private enterprise, the Congress cannot lose sight of the fact that in some areas Federal machinery is still required to enable small business to play its full part. . . . It is the best judgment of your committee that a more effective program for small business assistance at less cost to the taxpayers can be achieved by creating a new agency of the Federal government possessing the exact authority required to assist small business in making its full contribution to the national economic system. . ." Bills providing for such an agency were introduced. It would differ from its predecessors in that it would have broad scope to work exclusively in be-half of small business of all kinds, in all times, and it would be empowered with the authority to make loans, guide federal procurement, provide management training, and be the advocate of small business.

The policy was to be: "The essence of the American economic system of private enterprise is free competition. Only through full and free competition can free markets, free entry into business, and opportunities for the expression and growth of personal initiative and individual judgment be assured. The preservation and expansion of such competition is basic, not only to the economic well-being, but to the security of this Nation. Such security and well-being cannot be realized unless the actual and potential capacity of small business is encouraged and developed. It is the declared policy of the Congress that the Government should aid, counsel, assist, and protect insofar as is possible the interest of small business concerns. . ."

Hearings began in mid-May, 1953, and were relatively brief, with minimum opposition from within the federal establishment or from the private sector. Conflicts between the Senate and House bills were ironed out and the result passed by voice vote. The RFC would be dissolved. A "Small Business Administration" would have an opportunity to determine the usefulness of this agency. The bill, which became Public Law 83-163, was signed by President Eisenhower on July 30, and the SBA was born.

The fundamental purposes of the Small Business Administration (SBA) are to: aid, counsel, assist, and protect the interests of small business; insure that small business concerns receive a fair proportion of government purchases, contracts, and subcontracts, as well as of the sales of government property; make loans to small business concerns, state and local development companies, and the victims of floods or other catastrophes; license, regulate, and make loans to small business investment companies; improve the management skills of small business owners, potential owners, and managers; and conduct studies of the economic environment.

The Small Business Administration was created by the Small Business Act of 1953 (67 Stat. 384; 15 U.S.C. 631 et seq.), as amended. It also derives its authority from the Small Business Investment Act of 1958 (72 Stat. 689; 15 U.S.C. 661), as amended, title IV of the Economic Opportunity Act of 1964 (78 Stat. 526, as amended; 42 U.S.C. 2901 et seq.), and the Disaster Relief Act of 1970 (84 Stat. 1744; 42 U.S.C. 4401 et seq.). The secretary of commerce has delegated to the administration certain responsibilities and functions under section 202 of the Public Works and Economic Development Act of 1965 (79 Stat. 556; 42 U.S.C. 3142).

Functions and Activities

Financial Assistance. The Small Business Administration provides financial counseling, and loan guarantees, in addition to making direct or lender participation loans to small business concerns to help them finance plant construction, con-

57

version, or expansion; the acquisition of equipment, facilities, machinery, supplies, or materials; and, if necessary, provide them with working capital. Revolving lines of credit are also available to small businesses. The agency makes, participates in, or guarantees economic opportunity loans made under provisions contained in title IV of the Economic Opportunity Act. Included under this program is special assistance for Vietnam-era veterans.

The victims of floods, riots, civil disorders, and other catastrophes are provided with loans to aid them in repairing, rebuilding, or replacing their homes, businesses, or other property. Loans are provided to assist small businesses: that have sustained substantial economic injury resulting from a major disaster or such natural disaster as excessive rainfall or drought; that have been economically injured by a federally-aided urban renewal or highway construction pro-fram, or by any construction program conducted with Federal funds; or that may suffer economic injury as the result of meeting requirements of the Occupational Safety and Health Act, the Egg Products Inspection Act, the Wholesome Meat Act, and the Poultry Products Act; as well as to those that have suffered economic injury as a result of their inability to process or market a product for human consumption because of disease or toxicity occurring in the product through natural or undetermined causes.

Loans are also made to help small coal mines meet standards set by the Coal Mine Health and Safety Act of 1969. In 1972, the agency was authorized to make loans to assist small firms meet federal water pollution standards and to make special loans to handicapped individuals and nonprofit organizations producing goods or services by the handicapped.

Under provisions of Sections 501 and 502 of the Small Business Investment Act, loans are made by state and local development companies. The agency also guarantees the payment of rentals under leases entered into by small business concerns and guarantees to surety companies up to 90 percent of losses incurred on surety bonds issued to small contractors.

Procurement and Management Assistance. The Small Business Administration works closely with purchasing agencies of the federal government and with the nation's leading contractors in developing policies and procedures that will increase the number of contracts going to small business.

The SBA provides a wide range of services to small firms

to help them obtain and fulfill government contracts and sub-contracts. The agency can enter into government prime contracts and arrange to subcontract to small business concerns; and provides an appeal procedure for a low-bidding small firm whose ability to perform a contract is questioned by the contracting officer. It develops subcontract opportunities for small businesses by maintaining close contact with prime contractors and referring qualified small firms to them. SBA cooperates with other government agencies to channel a fair share of their sales of surplus property and resources to small business. The agency counsels interested small firms on the major aspects of importing and exporting, and works with other agencies to generate export activity and opportunities.

The agency cosponsors courses and conferences, prepares informational leaflets and booklets, and encourages research into the management problems of small business concerns. It counsels and conducts management workshops and courses for established as well as prospective businessmen and enlists the volunteer aid of retired and active executives to assist small businessmen to overcome their management problems.

Investment Assistance. For the purpose of improving and stimulating the national economy and the small business segment, the Small Business Administration licenses, regulates, and provides financial assistance to small business investment companies (SBICs), and minority enterprise small business investment companies (MESBICs). The sole function of these investment companies is to provide advisory services and venture capital in the form of equity financing and long term loan funds to small business concerns.

Planning, Research, and Analysis. SBA conducts economic and statistical research into matters affecting the competitive strength of small business. It conducts economic studies with emphasis on current and future opportunities, problems, and needs of small business. It researches the effect of federal laws, programs, and regulations on small business, and makes recommendations to federal agencies for appropriate adjustments to meet the needs of small business. SBA also analyzes the economic and social effects of its own activities, and prepares recommendations on long-term legislative requirements. The agency participates in the government-wide planning programing and budgeting systems, and in this connection it develops 5-year plans outlining resource requirements for the

59

agency.

SBA conducts industry studies and develops size definitions for the major agency assistance programs. It recommends and promulgates size standards; processes size inquirees received from various companies and members of Congress, and conducts industry hearings on size matters.

The administration maintains liaison with universities and other groups conducting research and studying economic factors pertaining to small business, and furnishes economic and statistical information to aid them in carrying out those studies.

Emphasis is placed on the application of economic analyses to the problem of allocating the agency's resources among its programs and field offices to obtain the maximum benefit to the small business community and achieve agency objectives.

How to Use the Small Business Administration. Most small independent businesses -- except gambling or speculative firms, newspapers, television, radio stations and other forms of media -- are eligible for SBA assistance.

For purposes of making loans, SBA defines a small business as one that meets these general size standards:

a) Wholesale -- annual receipts from $5 million to $15 million depending on the industry.

b) Retail or Service -- annual receipts from $1 million to $5 million, depending on the industry.

c) Construction -- annual receipts of not more than $5 million, averaged over a three-year period.

d) Manufacturing -- from 250 to 1,500 employees depending on the industry.

More detailed definitions are set forth in Section 121.3-10 of Part 121, Chapter I, Title 13 of the Code of Federal Regulations.

Business Loans

When a small businessman with a financial problem comes to SBA for advice and assistance, agency loan officers review his problem and suggest possible courses of action. If he needs money and cannot borrow it on reasonable terms, SBA often can help. The agency will consider either participating with a bank in a loan or guaranteeing up to 90 percent of the loan. If a bank or other lending institution cannot provide the funds, SBA will consider lending the entire amount as a direct government loan if funds are available. However, most of SBA's loans are made in cooperation with banks.

SBA looks at past earning records and future prospects of a small businessman to determine whether he has the ability to repay a loan, and any other fixed debts, out of business profits. SBA loans may be used for: business construction, expansion or conversion; purchase of machinery, equipment, facilities, supplies or materials; or working capital.

Direct and Immediate Participation Loans. SBA, at present, can make a direct loan up to $100,000 unless funds are not available. In participation loans, the SBA and the private lending institution each put up part of the funds immediately. The maximum interest rate on SBA's share is 5-1/2 percent. The bank may set a legal and reasonable rate, but SBA's share may not be in excess of $150,000 in any immediate participation loan at this time.

Loan Guaranty Plan. SBA can guarantee up to 90 percent or $350,000, whichever is less of a bank loan, to a small firm for the same purposes as direct and participation loans. The interest rate is set by the bank, within certain limits set by SBA from time to time.

Pool Loans. SBA makes loans to corporations that are formed and capitalized by groups of small business companies for purchasing raw materials, equipment, inventory or supplies to use in their individual businesses. These loans may also be made to obtain the benefits of research and development or to establish R&D facilities.

The agency, alone or with a bank, may lend as much as $250,000 for each pool member. The SBA interest rate is 5 percent, and the maturity may be up to 10 years. However, when these loans are used for construction, maximum maturity may be for as long as twenty years.

Economic Opportunity Loans. Economic Opportunity Loans make it possible for the disadvantaged businessman or woman who has the capability and the desire to own their own businesses. Both prospective and established small businesses may receive assistance under this program.

The Economic Opportunity Loan Program provides both financial and management assistance. The maximum amount is $50,000 for up to fifteen years.

Any resident of the United States, Puerto Rico, and Guam may apply for an EOL if:

61

1 - Total family income from all sources (other than welfare) is not sufficient for the basic needs of that family; or

2 - Due to social or economic disadvantage he or she has been denied the opportunity to acquire adequate business financing through normal lending channels on reasonable terms. This includes honorably-discharged Vietnam-era veterans.

Every applicant must show that he has the ability to operate a business successfully and that the loan can be repaid from the earnings of the business.

Although character and ability are more important than collateral under this program, every applicant is expected to have some of his own money or other assets invested in the business.

Development Company Loans. SBA believes that a vigorous national economy depends on the ability of each local community to develop its own economy. Throughout the nation, local communities are finding that they can increase job opportunities, and boost individual income and local tax revenues by helping business concerns get started, diversify, expand their operations, and modernize their facilities. This agency has two development-company lending programs.

SBA makes loans to state development companies to supply long-term loans and equity capital to small business concerns. The SBA may lend a state development company as much as the company's total outstanding borrowing from all other sources. These loans may be for as long as twenty years at variable interest rates. A state development company is a corporation organized by a special act of the state legislature, to operate state-wide to assist the growth and development of business concerns, including small businesses in its area.

Local development companies are made up of citizens whose primary purpose is to improve the local economy. They assist in the planned economic growth of the community by promoting and assisting the development of small business concerns in the area.

To be eligible for this kind of loan, citizens must put up their own personal dollars. As a corporation with at least 75 percent of its ownership vested in persons living or doing business in the community, local people assume responsibility for projects they sponsor. A local development company (LDC) may be organized as a profit or nonprofit corporation and must have a minimum of twenty-five stockholders or members.

A local development company must provide a reasonable share of the cost of the project, generally 20 percent of the total amount. A maximum of $350,000 may be borrowed from SBA for each identifiable small business to be assisted for as long as twenty-five years.

Development company loans may help: to buy land; build a new factory; acquire machinery and equipment; expand or convert existing facilities, provided the project will assist a specific small business.

The agency participates with banks, insurance companies, pension fund groups, other agencies, state authorities, commissions and others when making loans to local development companies.

Disaster Loans. In cases of disasters -- storms, floods, earthquakes, or other catastrophes -- the Small Business Administration can help victims repair physical damage or overcome economic injury. The agency makes loans to individuals, business concerns of all sizes, and nonprofit organizations to repair or replace damaged structures, lost or damaged furnishings, business machinery, equipment and inventory.

The agency may make a disaster loan with a bank or other private lending institution, or entirely on its own. The amount of a loan is determined generally by the loss, the needs of the applicant, and other factors. Under a physical disaster, the amount may not exceed $50,000 for homes, $10,000 for furniture and fixtures, but not to exceed $55,000 repair or replacement of homes and household goods; and up to $500,000 for rehabilitation of businesses. Loans may be for as long as thirty years.

When a bank-SBA loan is made, the bank may charge its regular interest rates within certain limits set by SBA from time to time. However, the agency sets its share at a low interest rate set by statute.

The SBA works closely with the American Red Cross in disaster areas, coordinating its loan program with the Red Cross grant program.

In areas hit by major or natural disasters, determined by the president or the secretary of agriculture, small firms suffering economic losses are eligible for SBA loans. SBA funds may be used to provide working capital and pay financial obligations (except bank loans) that the borrower would

63

have been able to meet if not for the disaster.

The interest rate on SBA's share of a bank–SBA loan or a loan made entirely by the agency is set by the secretary of the treasury. A participating bank may set the rate on its share within limits set by SBA from time to time.

SBA also makes loans to small firms that have suffered substantial economic injury because they cannot process or market a product for human consumption because of disease or toxicity resulting from either natural or undetermined causes. This is know as "product disaster."

The interest rate is set by the secretary of the treasury on SBA's share of a bank-SBA loan, or a loan made entirely by the agency. A participating bank may place the rate on its own share within limits set by SBA from time to time.

Small firms with substantial economic injury as a result of being displaced by or being near federally-aided urban renewal and other construction projects are eligible to apply for SBA loans to help relocate or re-establish. Reasonable upgrading of the business while re-establishing is permitted. These are "displaced business" loans.

The interest rate is established yearly according to statutory formula. A bank may set the interest rate on its share within reasonable limits.

Coal Mine Health and Safety Loans. A loan may be made to assist any small business concern operating a coal mine that must make changes in its equipment, facilities, or operations in order to meet the standards set by the Federal Coal Mine Health and Safety Act of 1969, if SBA determines that the concern is likely to suffer substantial economic injury without a loan. The Bureau of Mines will make an inspection of the small firm, and if it does not measure up to the requirements set out in the Federal Coal Mine Health and Safety Act, the Bureau then issues a notice of deficiency. The amount and use of the loan needed to correct these deficiencies are based on the notice received from the Bureau of Mines.

Consumer Protection Loans. SBA may make a loan to any small business concern that must make changes in its equipment, facilities, or operation in order to meet the requirements of the Egg Products Act, the Wholesome Poultry Products Act, and the Wholesome Meat Act of 1967, if the SBA determines that such a concern is likely to suffer substantial economic injury without the loan. The U.S. Department of Agriculture or the appropriate state authority will issue a list of required changes based on its inspection of the premises to determine the amount and use of the necessary loan.

Occupational Safety and Health. A loan may be made to assist a small business firm that must make changes in its equipment, facilities, or operations in order to comply with Federal standards under the Occupational Safety and Health Act of 1970, or State standards adopted pursuant to this legislation, if SBA determines that the firm is likely to suffer substantial economic injury without a loan. A loan applicant may be considered under either of the following:

1 - Voluntary Compliance Procedure -- when a small business concern independently initiates changes in order to comply with federal standards.

2 - Cited Violation Procedure -- when a small business concern is required by the OSH Administration to undertake action in order to meet federal or state standards.

Lease Guarantee Program. Small businessmen often are unable to lease good locations because they do not have top credit ratings required by landlords. SBA, in certain cases, will issue an insurance policy or reinsure a policy issued by a private insurance company that guarantees the rent for a small businessman. When private insurance participation is not available, SBA may guarantee the leases directly. The guarantee may extend for a minimum of five years to a maximum of twenty years on a participating basis, and ten to twenty years on a direct basis.

Premiums are based on actuarial studies and are payable in advance with no refunds. Although the small businessman is required to pay three months rent in advance to be held in escrow in case of rent defaults, it will be returned to him when his lease is up, with 4 percent interest, if there are no defaults. In some cases, the landlord may agree to a three-month deductible clause in the policy in lieu of the escrowed rent.

Applicants for lease guarantee policies are evaluated under a risk analysis system devised specifically for the SBA program. Under this system, the applicant's management skills, his financial position, the location in which he wishes to rent, and his business are analyzed.

The agency is seeking to widen small business participation in this program, which can be valuable to small firms trying to relocate or trying to obtain prime space.

Surety Bond Program. The Small Business Administration

is committed to help make the bonding process more accessible to small and emerging contractors who, for whatever reasons, might have found bonding previously unavailable to them. SBA is authorized to guarantee to a qualified surety up to 90 percent of losses incurred under bid, payment, or performance bonds issued to contractors on contracts valued up to $500,000. The contracts may be for construction, supplies or services provided by either a prime or subcontractor for governmental or nongovernmental work.

Applications for this assistance are available from any SBA field office. They are forwarded to the surety underwriters by an insurance agent with whatever credit, financial, and experience data is required by the surety company. After the surety's decision that the bond can be issued, subject to SBA's guarantee, a single-page agreement form is forwarded to the nearest SBA regional office by the surety company. The contractor pays SBA a small fee for this assistance, and the surety pays SBA a portion of its bond fee for the guarantee.

In order to be eligible for this program, the contractual situation must be included in the Contract Section of the Rating Manual of the Surety Association of America.

Minority Enterprise Program. SBA has combined its efforts with those of private industry, banks, local communities and the federal government to substantially increase the number of minority-owned, operated and managed businesses. For the first time in SBA history, the Minority Enterprise Program brings all the agency's services together in a coordinated thrust to make more sound business opportunities available to minority individuals.

Since minorities comprise 17 percent of the nation's population, yet own only 3-1/4 percent of the country's more than 8 million small businesses, the main objective of the Minority Enterprise Program consists of three supervisory units in SBA's Washington Headquarters office. ME field representatives are stationed in the regional offices, as well as in "outreach" offices located in areas with a heavy minority concentration. These representatives, cooperating with local community action groups, explain to potential minority entrepreneurs how all the services and programs of SBA are available to help them become successful business operators.

SBA tries to match minority individuals, who indicate a desire for business ownership and have some management aptitude, with sound business opportunities. The ME field representative then becomes the applicant's "advocate," advising and helping with financial statements, business projections, and any related material. Assistance is also given, if needed, in preparing a formal loan application.

The package service indicates the extent and type of management or technical assistance offered the applicant to help assure his business can be operated successfully. This phase of the program is emphasized because private surveys have shown consistently that faulty or inadequate management is responsible for more than 90 percent of new business failures.

ME loans are processed under relaxed eligibility criteria, with emphasis on the applicant's character and his ability to repay the loan and other obligations from the profits of the business.

The average ME loan is for approximately $28,000 and the average term of the loan is five to six years.

Most opportunities for minority businesses -- both new or established -- are in the retailing, distributing, franchising and service industries. Opportunities in these categories are not only greater in numbers, but usually require less equity capital on the part of the would-be owner.

SBA does, however, encourage and help minority and disadvantage individuals become owners of manufacturing firms, nursing homes, processing plants and similar businesses, whenever possible.

The agency counsels and, in many ways, assists minority groups in forming local development companies and specialized small business investment companies. Local development companies are formed by groups interested in stimulating the planned economic growth of their community by aiding small concerns in the local area. Specialized SBICs provide equity funds, long-term loans and management assistance to small business concerns owned by socially or economically disadvantaged persons.

The Minority Enterprise Program also has an active plan to help minority contractors locate and coordinate available help at all levels from public and private sources in order to grow and improve their productive capabilities.

Minority-owned or managed firms interested in performing government contracts are helped through Section 8(a) of the Small Business Act, under which SBA is authorized to act as prime contractor for certain types of goods and services and subcontract orders to individual small firms. The goal of the program is to open the doors of government contracting opportunities to minority businesses unable, or unlikely to get a chance to bid on competitive contracts.

Surety bond guarantees are made on construction contracts up to $500,000. The revolving line-of-credit program, designed to aid minority contractors, is now available to any small business with an assignable contract.

Based on SBA's experiences with the 8(a) program, the agency has developed a system called the Minority Vendors Program, whereby major private corporations are provided a service which will match their procurement needs with minority vendors qualified to satisfy those needs.

In all its ME activities, SBA works closely with other governmental agencies, trade associations, larger businesses, franchisors, and local civic and business organizations.

SCORE (Service Corps of Retired Executives), counselors, as well as SBA Advisory Council members across the country, also play an active role in supporting minority enterprise activities.

Small Business Investment Companies (SBICs). The SBA helps finance small firms through privately owned small business investment companies. SBICs are SBA-licensed companies which supply venture capital and long-term financing to small firms for expansion, modernization, and sound financing of their operations. They may also provide management assistance.

SBICs must operate within SBA regulations but their transactions with small companies are private arrangements and have no connection with SBA.

Initial minimum private investment required in an SBIC may vary from $150,000 to as much as $1 million, depending on the area to be served, the prospects for a sound, profitable operation, and whether or not businesses to be financed will be largely owned by persons whose participation in the free enterprise system is hampered because of social or economic disadvantages.

SBA may make loans, or guarantee 100 percent of the loans of private lending institutions, to SBICs to add to their funds for financing small firms. Such loans may be subordinated, with up to 15-year terms. Maximum loan to an SBIC is basically $15 million or twice the SBIC's private paid-in capital and paid-in surplus, whichever is smaller.

SBICs that specialize in venture capital financing and

are capitalized at more than $500,000 may qualify for SBA direct or SBA-guaranteed loans aggregating up to $20 million. Congress has authorized certain tax incentives to encourage more investment in SBICs.

SBA, in cooperation with the Department of Commerce, has instituted a specialized application of the SBIC principle wherein SBICs dedicated solely to assisting small business concerns owned and managed by socially or economically disadvantaged persons are organized under Section 301(d) of the Small Business Investment Act of 1958, as amended.

These SBICs are owned and operated by established industrial or financial concerns, community or business-oriented economic development organizations, or private or public investors to combine money and management resources for assistance to socially or economically disadvantaged entrepreneurs.

SBICs may make long-term loans, purchase stock or debt securities, or combine equity and loan financing. Minimum term of SBIC financing is five years, except that all SBICs may maintain up to one-half of its portfolio in investments in disadvantaged firms with minimum investment periods of thirty months.

For SBIC financing, a concern is small if its assets do not exceed $7-1/2 million, its net worth is not more than $2.5 million, and its 2-year average annual profits after federal income taxes did not exceed $250,000. A concern may also qualify under the regular business loan size standards.

Procurement Assistance. Each year, the federal government contracts for billions of dollars with private companies. SBA helps small businessmen obtain a share of this government business by providing several forms of assistance to small firms that want to obtain government prime contracts and related subcontracts.

Specialists in SBA field offices counsel small businessmen on prime contracting and subcontracting. They direct them to government agencies that buy the products or services they supply; help to get their names placed on bidders' lists; assist in obtaining drawings and specifications for proposed purchases and offer many other related services, which include supplying leads on research and development projects.

Prime Contracts Program. Major government purchasing agencies "set-aside" contracts or portions of contracts for small business bidding. SBA has its own procurement repre-

69

sentatives stationed in major military and civilian procurement installations. They recommend additional "set-asides," provide small business sources to contracting officers, assist small concerns with contracting problems and recommend relaxation of unduly restrictive specifications. SBA also checks the effectiveness of small business programs administered by procurement installations.

Certificates of Competency Program. If a small firm is low bidder on a federal contract and its ability to perform the contract is questioned by the contracting officer, the company may ask SBA for a Certificate of Competency (COC).

If the firm applies, SBA industrial specialist make an on-site study of its facilities, management, performance record and financial status. If SBA concludes that the company has, or can obtain, the necessary credit and production capacity to perform the contract successfully, it issues a certificate (COC) attesting to that fact. A COC is valid only for the specific contract for which it is issued and is binding on the contracting officer.

Subcontracting Program. The SBA develops subcontract opportunities for small business by maintaining close contact with prime contractors and referring qualified small firms to them.

SBA works closely with the largest contract-awarding agencies; the Department of Defense, General Services Administration, National Aeronautics and Space Agency and the Atomic Energy Commission, and sometimes others. Under regulations established by these agencies, government prime contractors must give small concerns an adequate opportunity to compete for their subcontracts.

Property Sales Program. Each year, the federal government sells large amounts of real and personal property and natural resources surplus to its programs. SBA cooperates with the General Services Administration, Department of Agriculture, Department of Interior, the Department of Defense and other government agencies to channel a fair share of this surplus property and resources to small business.

Contract Opportunity Meetings. In cooperation with local business groups and other government agencies, SBA participates in meetings where small businessmen can learn of prime contract and subcontract opportunities. Government contracting agencies and prime contractors present their needs and requirements, and discuss bidding opportunities.

SBA field offices can provide information about scheduled meetings.

Locating Additional Suppliers. SBA representatives are particularly watchful for purchases on which few small firms have bid in the past. If the representatives believe small firms can perform these contracts, SBA offices locate small companies that would be interested in bidding.

Another source of information and guidance to those who want to buy and sell to the government is "The U.S. Government Purchasing and Sales Directory." It lists principal goods and services bought by military and civilian agencies and the purchasing offices that buy them. It also tells where to obtain copies of the specifications used in government purchasing and provides helpful information on government sales of property. The Directory is sold by the Superintendent of Documents, U.S. Government Printing Office, Washington, D.C., 20402 and is available at many libraries.

"Selling to the U.S. Government," (OPI-12), another SBA publication, explains the government's buying methods and suggests steps to take in selling to it and to prime contractors. The leaflet is available free from all SBA offices.

Management Assistance. Most businesses fail for lack of good management. For this reason, SBA offers a diversified program of management and technical assistance to strengthen small firms and to improve their operations. Under SBA's program of management assistance, conferences, problem clinics, and individual counseling are offered so that the management ability of increasing numbers of small business owner-managers can be improved. The program is executed by Management Assistance Officers in the field offices, who pinpoint problems in operating, develop solutions, and help with planning.

SBA furnishes individual assistance to small businessmen with management problems, and also will counsel prospective small businessmen who want management assistance, or information on specific types of business enterprises.

In addition to staff professionals, small businessmen can benefit from the services of SCORE, and ACE (Active Corps of Executives), together with other national associations who lend individual help.

SBA draws from this pool of talent to match the need of the small businessman with the expertise of its volunteers. Then an assigned counselor visits the small businessman in his establishment. Through careful observation, he makes a detailed analysis of the business and its problems. If it is a complex problem, he may call on other volunteer experts to assist. Finally, he will offer a plan to remedy the trouble, and help the businessman through his critical period. This service is free, except for out-of-pocket expenses.

Chapter 8

TAX, INSURANCE, AND SAFETY CONSIDERATIONS

Taxes

Proper and adequate financial records are practically indispensable to intelligent business management. When such records are accurately kept and properly interpreted, they are an invaluable source of information to the proprietor of the business with respect to his operations. In addition, such records are necessary for the proper preparation of the various tax returns which must be made in connection with the business.

Because of the high rates involved, the federal income tax generally has a greater impact upon business than any other form of taxation. Such tax, however, affects varying types of business organizations in different ways.

A sole proprietor operating a business by himself will merely account for his business profit or loss on his own individual income tax return. Partnerships as such are not taxed on their income under the federal income tax provisions. However, they are required to file information returns, which disclose the partnership income and each partner's share of such income. The individual partners then include their respective separate shares of the partnership income in their own personal federal income tax returns.

A corporation, on the other hand, pays a separate federal income tax as an individual entity. In this regard it should be also kept in mind that on the whole the tax rates on corporations are generally somewhat higher than individual personal tax rates. Of course, in computing its net income for tax purposes, the corporation deducts all proper charges of operation. It can therefore deduct the reasonable salaries paid to its employees. In a closed corporation, when the individual stockholders ordinarily are on the payroll of the corporation as employees, their salaries are deducted before the corporation's net profit is determined, as long as the salaries are reasonable. Each individual who receives a salary from the corporation must include it in his personal income tax return.

With the corporate form of organization, the profits of the

business are paid out to the stockholders as dividends. When a corporation declares a dividend, the amounts received by the individual stockholders are to be included in their personal income tax returns. A dividend is not an item of operating cost to the corporation, and therefore, a corporation cannot deduct the amount of such dividends paid to its stockholders when it computes its own profit for tax purposes. Thus, in effect, such dividends may be taxed twice: the corporation first pays its own income tax upon its net profit, and thereafter when the profits are distributed to individual stockholders by way of dividends, the amounts so received must be included in the personal income tax returns of the stockholders.

Under federal income tax law, employers are required to deduct or withhold a part of the wages of each employee, to be applied against the individual income tax that the employee will have to pay for the year. This is part of the "pay as you go" plan for payment of federal income taxes, which was put into effect a number of years ago. There are several different methods of determining the amounts that an employer shall withhold in federal income taxes from the wages he pays his employees. The amount actually deducted depends upon the wages being earned, and the tax rate as prescribed at the particular time. The employer is required to keep accurate records in regard to withholding, and must pay over the monies collected regularly. At the end of the year, he must provide the employee with two copies of a form known as Form W-2. The employee attaches the original of this form to his own income tax return when he submits it to the income tax authorities. If the amount that was withheld by his employer turns out to be greater than the income tax for which the employee is responsible during the year, he receives a refund for the difference from the Treasury Department. If, on the other hand, his income tax is greater than the amount withheld, the withholding is applied against the tax due, and he is then required to pay the difference.

In addition to the federal income tax, most states also have income tax laws or their equivalents. The state income tax rates are ordinarily much lower than those of the federal government. In general, the state tax returns will be similar to those that are submitted to the federal government. However, they are generally not identical, and the differences between the various state and federal tax laws must be taken into account when the returns are actually prepared. In some states, corporations do not pay income taxes, but instead pay what are called franchise taxes, which, however, are in general computed upon the basis of the net profit made by the corporation during the year. Similarly many states have so-called unincorporated business taxes that are assessed against persons who do business in the noncorporate form.

Besides the income tax, the businessman today must cope with a wide variety of miscellaneous taxes that may be imposed upon his business. One of the most common is the sales tax, which is utilized by a great number of states and local municipalities for raising part of their revenue. In general, the tax is paid by the ultimate purchaser of the goods involved, but the seller is held responsible for the collection of the tax, and for turning over the sums collected by him to the particular governmental agency. Sales taxes are most prominent in connection with ordinary retail business.

Another type of taxation, which is common in practically all states, is the property tax, or some variation of it. Depending upon the locality involved, a businessman may be assessed on real property, or on personal property, or on so-called intangible property. Ordinarily the actual amount of the tax is small, and is computed on a percentage basis against the total value of the particular property in question held by the business. Somewhat similar is the occupancy tax, which many local communities assess against premises occupied for business purposes. Again, the actual amount of the tax is relatively small, computed on the total rental value of the premises so occupied.

There are, in addition, a large number of so-called excise taxes. Originally such taxes were generally intended to be levied against luxuries, but today many of the items that are taxed are necessities rather than luxuries. Excise taxes are levied against many items by the federal government, and in addition, the states have various forms of excise taxation. For example, gasoline is subject to a federal tax, and also to a state tax, practically uniformly throughout the country. Types of items upon which excise taxes are levied are cigarettes, telephone and telegraph bills, luggage, precious jewelry, amusement admissions, and many others. Again, these taxes are actually paid by the purchaser of the particular goods involved, but they must be collected by the seller, reported and turned over by him to the government.

Under the Federal Social Security Laws, taxes are also levied to provide funds for payment to employees in the form of old age benefits, and Unemployment Insurance. Insofar as the old age benefits are concerned, the tax is levied against both the employer and the employee. While not all employers are covered by the law, the tendency has been to continually widen the scope of the legislation to cover more and more persons. Self-employed persons may obtain coverage under the act in most instances.

The actual mechanism of the taxation with respect to Unemployment Insurance is somewhat more complicated. Whereas the provisions for old age benefits apply when only one employee is employed by the business, the Unemployment Insurance provisions vary from state to state. For example, in New York State, Unemployment Insurance is paid by all employers who have four or more employees. This amount is paid solely by the employer, and there is no deduction for Unemployment Insurance from the employee. If the employer has at least eight or more employees, then he pays an additional Unemployment Insurance Tax to the federal government.

The above summarizes the most important taxes that the businessman must know and the list is by no means all inclusive. There is a wide variety of license fees, occupational taxes, health insurance taxes, and others, which are levied by various agencies of our government. Clearly then, it is impossible to hope to account properly for all taxes unless the records maintained by the business are complete and accurate.

Insurance

It is beyond the scope of this volume to consider at length the detailed provisions of the various insurance contracts and policies that may be issued in connection with the ordinary business. It is important to recognize, however, that proper insurance coverage is an essential element of a good business operation. For this purpose, it is necessary to rely on the services of a competent and skilled insurance broker, preferably one with wide experience in the particular type of business to be covered.

As a practical matter, insurance may be even more important in some instances for a small business than it would be for a large one. A large enterprise is frequently in a position to absorb a loss that would financially embarrass or possibly even bankrupt a smaller company. Thus, a large corporation operating a fleet of hundreds of automobiles or trucks may find from its own experience that it is cheaper not to have theft insurance on the fleet, since the actual losses suffered from year to year are less than the cost of the insurance for coverage on the whole fleet. On the other hand, a small retail business with a single truck should cover it against loss or damage, since the hardship suffered, were the truck stolen or damaged, could be comparatively great, or impossible to survive.

There is an extremely wide and extensive range of policies that are available for business protection. Some of the more obvious types are fire, theft, and liability insurance. Policies of this type are generally in force for practically all types of business.

In addition, there ar many special types that may be useful or desirable in a particular branch of business. For example, credit insurance, (insuring against extensive losses resulting from bad debts), can be obtained and is extremely useful when the business does a large amount of credit work. In connection with retail stores that handle customers goods extensively, for example, shoe repair or tailor shops, so-called bailee insurance protecting against loss or damage to the customer's goods may be obtained. When the employees of the business handle large sums of money regularly, embezzlement or fidelity insurance may be placed to cover loss from this source.

In all states, Workmen's Compensation Insurance must be paid by the employer to insure against injuries to the employees. Workmen's Compensation is a statutory insurance mechanism for providing cash-wage benefits and medical care to victims of work-connected injuries. Typical features of a workmen's compensation act include:

a) the principle that an employee is automatically entitled to certain benefits whenever he suffers a personal injury by accident in the course of or arising out of his employment;

b) negligence and fault are relatively immaterial;

c) only those individuals classified as employees are included;

d) employee benefits include cash-wage support at approximately one-half to two-thirds of one's average weekly wage plus hospital and medical expenses;

e) the employee and his dependents waive the common-law right to sue the employer for damages for injuries covered by the act. Public liability insurance, covering accidents or injury to customers or to strangers, can be obtained from regularly established insurance companies.

In any event, it must be clear that insurance is such a broad subject that no general answer may be given as to the proper type of insurance to be placed without taking into consideration the particular requirements of the business involved, and the prospective cost of such insurance to the proprietor.

Safety

The businessman must consider the legal problems and requirements for safe working conditions. Recent state and federal laws have established strict guidelines for maintaining a safe environment for the employee. The Occupational Safety and Health Act of 1970 (P.L. 91-596), under the supervision and guidance of the National Institute for Occupational Safety and Health and the Department of Health, Education, and Welfare, is the primary program dealing directly with safety and health in the workplace. Under the Department of Labor the Occupational Safety and Health Administration (OSHA) was created to supervise and assist employers in achieving all necessary safety and health standards. The provisions of this law apply to every employer engaged in a business affecting commerce who has employees. OSHA program activities include establishing safety and health standards, enforcement, training, education, information, state program assistance, safety statistics, and executive direction and administration. Occupational Safety and Health Standards adopted under the Occupational Safety and Health Act and enforced by the Labor Department appear in Title 29, Chapter XVIII, Part 1910 of the Code of Federal Regulations. To locate the closest regional OSHA office for assistance, the businessman should consult the latest edition of the United States Government Manual generally available in all libraries.

Chapter 9

THE SETTING OF PRICES

Generally, the owner of a business has had the right to establish the price at which he would sell his merchandise. He could determine his own markups, set his own credit terms, and if he so desired, even sell the product below what it actually cost him. However, recent economic problems confronting this country have resulted in certain federal statutory powers being authorized whereby the president has been able to exercise certain economic controls over prices and wages. In addition, state and federal price controls are recognized at law as valid when the public health, safety, and general welfare are at stake and when the controlling agency does not act in an arbitrary, discriminatory, or unreasonable manner. The exercise of the power to establish, fix, or regulate prices requires clear, explicit, and unambiguous language in the statute.

Absent a statute to the contrary, a businessman may dispose of his property or his services at any price agreed upon betweeen the merchant and purchaser. Price cutting is not ordinarily unfair competition and can be regarded as a legitimate competitive practice unless made unlawful by a statute such as the Fair Trade Law or the Uniform Consumer Credit Code (deceptive sales practices). Price cutting may constitute unfair competition when perpetrated, not for the purpose of promoting one's own business ends, but for the purpose of inflicting injury on a competitor, especially when there is an inaccurate and misleading representation regarding the goods, or where the product was advertised below cost without the ability or intent of the merchant to meet the demand stimulated. One should not cut his prices for the purpose of injuring a competitor.

Under a federal statute, the Clayton Act as amended by the Robinson-Patman Act, 15 U.S.C.A. § 13, it is unlawful for a person engaged in commerce to discriminate with prices among different purchasers of goods of like grade and quality, when the result may be to substantially lessen competition or to tend to create a monopoly. A violation of this statute results when price discrimination injures or prevents competition with the one who gives or receives such price advantages. For price discrimination to exist, there must be sales to two or more individuals. However, a refusal to sell is not a price discrimination under the statute. Price discrimination is lawful when it is based on real differences in grade, quality, or quantity, but is unlawful if based on fictional or artificial criteria. Purchasers, as well as sellers, are charged with responsibility for unlawful price discrimination. It is, however, a proper defense to a charge of price discrimination to assert that the lower price was made in good faith to meet an equally low price of a competitor.

The sale of an article under the Robinson-Patman Act is unlawful if sold at unreasonably low prices for the purpose of destroying a competitor. Price cutting is not in violation of the statute unless made for the purpose of discriminating among buyers. Thus a businessman has the right to sell his products at prices he establishes unless his price cutting is destructive or restrains trade.

Following the enactment of the Robinson-Patman Act, many states passed Unfair Practices Acts for the purpose of regulating business as a whole by preventing selling practices that the legislature had determined to be unfair. Most statutes were created to prevent ruinous price cutting and use of the "loss leader" as a form of merchandising. Generally, these statutes have been construed by the courts as not prohibiting ordinary sales below cost except when an intent to injure or destroy a competitor is clear. Relief, awarded under most statutes, is either injunctive, or an action for damages, or, under some statutes, a criminal prosecution. The businessman will want to consult closely with his lawyer before entering into a prolonged price war with his competition.

Under the common law it was a general rule that a contract was invalid if in it the seller of goods attempted to fix prices at which the merchandise could be resold. But modern day economics resulted in most states adopting fair trade statues that permited manufacturers to enter into contracts that fixed the resale prices for trademarked or trade named commodities. Such statutes are generally held to be lawful and not in violation of state and federal constitutional provisions.

The fair trade laws, by their nature, apply only to products that have a brand name or trade-mark. Indeed, the purpose of these statutes is to insure that quality standards will be observed in the sale of such products. The general scheme of the fair trade laws permits a manufacturer to determine in advance the minimum resale prices at which he wants his articles to be resold by the persons with whom he deals. When the manufacturer has determined such a price, he may then enter into a contract with the retailer, whereby the latter agrees that he will observe the set price. As a practical matter, it would be impossible for a large manufacturer to enter into such agreements with the thousands and thousands of retail distributors selling his product. To cover this situation, the statutes have generally provided that it is unnecessary for the manufacturer to enter into an agreement with all of his retail distributors; it is sufficient for him to enter into an agreement with any one distributor in the state, and thereafter gives notice of that fact to his other distributors. Under the statutes, the giving of such notice to the other distributors has the effect of the manufacturer entering into separate agreements with each distributor. In other words, the retailer who receives such a notice from the manufacturer is bound to observe the minimum resale prices set just as if he had actually entered into a separate agreement with the manufacturer providing the statute does not violate state or federal constitutional limitations.

By their nature, resale price maintenance statutes are especially pertinent in certain types of business, such as, the patent medicine and electrical appliance fields. In the food business, very little effort has been made to apply resale price maintenance, even when the products are branded or trade-marked.

To the extent that the statutes and agreements are in effect, they restrict the prices that the retailer can charge by setting a minimum. Technically, the statutes do not fix maximum prices. However, except in rare situations, the effect of setting a minimum price regulates both minimum and maximum prices, since it is extremely difficult for any retailer to charge more than the minimum price fixed by the manufacturer. His customers become so accustomed to paying the minimum fixed price that they would naturally balk at paying anything more.

The enforcement of retail price maintenance agreements is largely in the hands of the manufacturer. He can effectively stop any retailer who does not abide by the set prices, by refusing to sell to him any longer. At times, however, this does not give the manufacturer effective relief and in such situations he may seek court aid to obtain an injunction to prevent the retailer from cutting prices, and may even seek damages when he has suffered as a result.

Another factor, which is frequently overlooked in discussing what prices may be charged, is taxation. Today most municipalities and states depend upon a sales tax for the raising of revenue. In addition, there are a large number of excise taxes, both state and federal. For example, a large portion of the final selling price of cigarettes and gasoline is composed of the taxes imposed upon these products. Of course, all taxes must be taken into account when the final price is computed.

Lastly, economic conditions and inflation resulted in Congress passing the Economic Stabilization Act of 1970, P.L. 91-379, 84 Stat. 800; as amended by Act of December 17, 1970, P.L. 92-8; as amended by Act of May 18, 1971, P.L. 92-15; as amended by Act of 1971, P.L. 92-210; as amended by Economic Stabilization Act Amendments of 1973, April 30, 1973, P.L. 93-28. The purpose of the Act is to stabilize the economy, reduce inflation, and minimize unemployment by stabilizing prices, rents, wages, salaries, dividends and interests. It is not the purpose of this volume to explore this rapidly changing Act in detail. It is essential, however, that the businessman comprehend the scope and impact of this statute especially in regard to prices. Price controls are administered by the Price Commission and the Internal Revenue Service with the assistance of special boards and committees. Businesses are sometimes required to show that their prices are in compliance with the guidelines of the stabilization program. The rules for price controls are found in the law itself, in the regulations and rulings of the Cost of Living Council, the Price Commission, and the Internal Revenue Service. Close consultation with one's lawyer and with the agencies aforementioned is essential.

Chapter 10

THE CONSUMER

Commanding the attention of every businessman today is a powerful force -- consumerism. Although simple in name, it is complex in scope adding new dimensions to production and marketing standards for products and services. Today's businesses must accept new and enlarged responsibilities never before anticipated: production must be safe and durable; advertising and labeling must be accurate and complete; promotions can no longer be merely sales gimmicks but must comply with disclosure and fairness requirements. Sales responsibilities now extend beyond the sale date through the simply-worded guarantee, extended warranty protection, fair credit regulations, and environmental concerns. All states except Louisiana have afforded various protections to its consuming citizens through enactment of the Uniform Commercial Code. In addition, many states are codifying consumer credit protection through enactment of such statutes as the Uniform Consumer Credit Code. As of January 1, 1974, the following states had passed this increasingly popular statute: Colorado, Idaho, Indiana, Kansas, Oklahoma, Utah, and Wyoming. Federal law also assists the consumer, especially in the credit areas, through acts such as the Consumer Credit Protection Act, 15 U.S.C. 1601-1681t (Chapter 41).

Consumerism does not change the goal of a business to successfully produce and market a product or service. It does require the businessman to look anew at his production techniques, advertising methods, promotional devices, and selling format to see if they fairly represent the product in question and conform to all laws. The end result will be a more efficient and profitable utilization of business resources benefitting both the buyer and seller. President Nixon said in his October 30, 1969, message to Congress:

> To their credit, producers and sellers have generally become far more responsible with the passing years, but even the limited abuses which occur now have greater impact. Products themselves are more complicated; there is more about them that can go wrong and less about

them that can be readily understood by laymen. Mass production and mass distribution systems mean that a small error can have a wide effect; the carelessness of one producer can bring harm or disappointment to many. Moreover, the responsibility for a particular problem is far more difficult to trace than was once the case, and even when responsibility for an error can be assigned, it is often difficult to lodge an effective complaint against it.

All too often, the real advantages of mass production are accompanied by customer alienation; many an average buyer is intimidated by seemingly monolithic organizations and frequently comes to feel alone and helpless in what he regards as a cruelly impersonal market place. In addition, many of the government's efforts to help the consumer are still geared to the problems of past decades; when it is able to act at all, government too often acts too slowly.

Fortunately, most businessmen in recent years have recognized that the confidence of the public over a long period of time is an important ingredient for their own success and have themselves made important voluntary progress in consumer protection. At the same time, buyers are making their voices heard more often, as individuals and through consumer organizations. These trends are to be encouraged and our governmental programs must emphasize their value. Government consumer programs, in fact, are a complement to these voluntary efforts. They are designed to help honest and conscientious businessmen by discouraging their dishonest or careless competitors.

Thus, any new businessman will want to keep abreast of the entire consumer movement. Detailed self-studies and preventive management can stop many consumer complaints before they arise. Compliance with governmental regulations and fair-mindedness are essential modern business guides. Caveat emptor is no longer a maxim of the marketplace.

In conclusion, the businessman will want to become aware of the courts of limited jurisdiction located in his state. Called small claims courts in many locals, these forums were often used in the past by businesses to collect debts and enforce claims against customers, particularly those in low-income areas. Characteristic of these courts is the limitation of claims to not more than $300.00 and the requirement that no lawyers be present to represent the parties. Today, most statutes have been revised to restrict the number of occasions one might appear before these courts. The result is to make this type of court a more effective device for the consumer to seek relief for a poor product sold or an ineffective service rendered, and less of a collection agent for the merchant. The following is a sample small claims court statute indicating the scope and jurisdiction of this type of forum:

Ch. 239, §§ 1-12, (1973) Session Laws of Kansas 867.

Be it enacted by the Legislature of the State of Kansas:

Section 1. This act shall be known and may be cited as the "small claims procedure act."

Sec. 2. This act shall apply to and be an alternative procedure for the processing of small claims in courts of limited jurisdiction, and the provisions of this act shall be part of and supplemental to the code of civil procedure before courts of limited jurisdiction, and any acts amendatory thereof or supplemental thereto. Except as otherwise specifically provided or where a different or contrary provision is included in this act, the code of civil procedure before courts of limited jurisdiction shall be applicable to the processing of small claims and judgments under this act.

Sec. 3. As used in this act:

(a) "Small claim" means a claim for the recovery of money or personal property, where the amount claimed or the value of the property sought does not exceed three hundred dollars ($300), exclusive of interest and costs. In actions of replevin, the verified petition fixing the value of the property shall be determinative of the value of the property for jurisdictional purposes. A "small claim" shall not include:

(1) An assigned claim;

(2) A claim based on an obligation or indebtedness allegedly owed to a person other than the person filing the claim, where the person filing the claim is not a full-time salaried employee of the person to whom the obligation or indebtedness is allegedly owed; or

85

(3) A claim obtained through subrogation.

(b) "Person" means an individual, partnership, corporation, fiduciary, joint venture, society, organization or other association of persons.

Sec. 4. An action seeking the recovery of a small claim shall be commenced by a person filing a written statement of his small claim with the clerk of the court, if service of process is obtained, or the first publication is made for service by publication, within ninety (90) days after the small claim is filed; otherwise, the action is deemed commenced at the time of service of process or first publication. An entry of appearance shall have the same effect as service. Upon the filing of plaintiff's small claim, the clerk of the court shall require from the plaintiff a deposit of five dollars ($5), plus publication costs, if any, as security for costs in the action, unless for good cause shown the judge shall waive such requirement. No person may file more than five (5) small claims under this act in the same court during any calendar year.

Sec. 5. It is the purpose of this act to provide and maintain simplicity of pleading, and the court shall supply the forms prescribed by this act to assist the parties in preparing their pleadings. The only pleading required in an action commenced under this act shall be the statement of plaintiff's claim, which shall be on the form prescribed by this act and be denominated a petition, except that a defendant who has a claim against the plaintiff, which arises out of the transaction or occurrence that is the subject matter of the plaintiff's claim, shall file a statement of his claim on the form prescribed by this act. The court shall not have any jurisdiction under this act to hear or determine any claim by a defendant which does not arise out of the transaction or occurrence which is the subject matter of plaintiff's claim.

No pleadings other than those provided for herein shall be allowed. It shall be sufficient that each pleading set forth a short and plain statement of the claim, showing that the pleader is entitled to relief, and contain a demand for judgment for the relief to which the pleader deems himself entitled.

Sec. 6. (a) Whenever a plaintiff demands judgment beyond the scope of the small claims jurisdiction of the court, the court shall either: (1) Dismiss the action without prejudice at the cost of the plaintiff; (2) allow the plaintiff to amend his pleadings and service of process to bring his demand for judgment within the scope of the court's small claims jurisdiction and thereby waive his right to recover any excess, assessing the costs accrued to the plaintiff; or (3) if the plaintiff's demand for judgment is within the scope of the court's general jurisdiction, allow the plaintiff to amend his pleadings and service of process so as to commence an action in such court in compliance with K.S.A. 1972 Supp. 61-1703, assessing the costs accrued to the plaintiff.

(b) Whenever a defendant asserts a claim beyond the scope of the court's small claims jurisdiction, but within the scope of the court's general jurisdiction, the court may determine the validity of defendant's entire claim. If the court refuses to determine the entirety of any such claim, the court must allow the defendant to: (1) Make no demand for judgment and reserve the right to pursue his entire claim in a court of competent jurisdiction; (2) make demand for judgment of that portion of his claim not exceeding three hundred dollars ($300) and reserve the right to bring an action in a court of competent jurisdiction for any amount in excess thereof; or (3) make demand for judgment of that portion of his claim not exceeding three hundred dollars ($300) and waive his right to recover any excess.

Sec. 7. (a) The trial of all actions shall be by the court, and no party in any such action shall be represented by an attorney prior to judgment. Discovery methods or proceedings shall not be allowed; nor shall the taking of depositions for any purpose be permitted. No order of attachment or garnishment shall be issued in any action commenced under this act prior to judgment in such action.

(b) Any judgment entered under this act on a claim which is not a small claim, as defined in section 3, or which has been filed with the court in contravention of the limitation prescribed by section 4 on the number of claims which may be filed by any person, shall be void and unenforceable.

Sec. 8. The venue of actions commenced under this act shall be as prescribed in article 19 of chapter 61

of the Kansas Statutes Annotated, except that, without
some other basis for venue being present, the county in
which the cause of action arose shall not be proper venue
for an action against a resident of this state.

Sec. 9. No appeal shall be taken by either party unless
the appellant shall file a supersedeas bond in the manner
prescribed by K.S.A. 1972 Supp. 61-2105.

Sec. 10. The costs of any action commenced in a
court of limited jurisdiction under this act shall be taxed
against the parties as in other actions in such court. If
the appellee is successful on appeal, the district court
shall award to the appellee, as part of the costs, reasonable attorneys' fees incurred by him on appeal.

Sec. 11. Subject to the approval of the governing
body of the political subdivision which pays the salary
of the judge of the court of limited jurisdiction situated
therein, such judge may appoint a judge pro tem to hear and
determine the actions commenced under this act. Said
judge pro tem shall hold court at such times and places as
may be directed by the judge, consistent insofar as prac-
ticable with the provisions of K.S.A. 1972 Supp. 61-1605,
and he shall receive such compensation for his services
as may be prescribed by said governing body.

Sec. 12. It is the purpose of this act to provide a
forum for the speedy trial of small claims, and to this
end, the court may make such orders or rulings, consistent with the provisions of this act, as are necessary
to promote justice and fairly protect the parties.

Appendix A

JURISDICTIONS ADOPTING THE UNIFORM PARTNERSHIP ACT

(as of December, 1972)

Jurisdiction	Laws	Effective Date	Statutory Citation
Alabama.	1971, No. 1513	1-1-1972	Code of Ala., Tit. 43, §§ 5(1) to 5(43).
Alaska	1917, c. 69	5-3-1917*	AS 32.05.010-32.05.430.
Arizona.	1954, c. 66	3-25-1954*	A.R.S. §§ 29-201 to 29-244.
Arkansas	1941, Act 263	3-26-1941*	Ark. Stats. §§ 65-101 to 65-143.
California	1949, p. 674	5-23-1949*	West's Ann.Corp.Code, §§ 15001-15045.
Colorado	1931, c. 129	4-17-1931*	C.R.S. '53, 104-1-1 to 104-1-43.
Connecticut.	1961, No. 158	5-15-1961	C.G.S.A. §§ 34-39 to 34-82.
Delaware	1947, c. 229	4-8-1947*	6 Del.C. §§ 1501-1543.
Dist. of Columbia. .	1962, 76 Stat. 636	9-27-1962*	D.C.C.E. § 41-301 et seq.
Florida.	1972, c. 72-108	1-1-1973	F.S.A. §§ 620.56 to 620.77.
Guam			Guam Civil Code, §§ 2395-2472.
Idaho.	1919, c. 154	1-1-1920	I.C., §§ 53-301 to 53-343.
Illinois	1917, p. 625	7-1-1917	S.H.A., ch. 106 1/2, §§ 1-43.
Indiana.	1949, c. 114	1-1-1950	I.C. 1971, 23-4-1-1 to 23-4-1-43

*Date of Approval.

89

Jurisdiction	Laws	Effective Date	Statutory Citation
Iowa.	1971, (64 G.A.) S.F. 460	7-1-1971	I.C.A. §§ 544.1 to 544.43.
Kansas.	1972 c. 210	3-17-1972*	K.S.A. 56-301 et seq.
Kentucky.	1954, c. 38	3-24-1954*	KRS 362.150-362.360.
Maryland.	1916, c. 175	6-1-1916	Code 1957, art. 73A, §§ 1-43.
Massachusetts .	1922, c. 486	1-1-1923	M.G.L.A., c. 108A §§ 1-44.
Michigan.	1917, No. 72	4-17-1917*	M.C.L.A., §§ 449.1-449.43n.
Minnesota	1921, c. 487	6-1-1921	M.S.A. §§ 323.01-323.43.
Missouri.	1949, p. 506	8-9-1949*	V.A.M.S. §§ 358.010-358.430.
Montana	1947, c. 251	3-8-1947*	R.C.M.1947, §§ 63-101 to 63-515.
Nebraska.	1943, c. 143	5-25-1943*	R.R.S.1943, §§ 67-301 to 67-343.
Nevada.	1931, c. 74	7-1-1931	N.R.S. 87.010 to 87.430.
New Jersey. . . .	1919, c. 212	4-15-1919*	N.J.S.A. 42:1-1 to 42:1-43.
New Mexico. . . .	1947, c. 37	3-3-1947*	1953 Comp. §§ 66-1-1 to 66-1-43.
New York.	1919, c. 408	10-1-1919	McKinney's Partnership Law, §§ 1-74.
North Carolina. .	1941, c. 374	3-15-1941	G.S. §§ 59-31 to 59-73.
North Dakota. . .	1959, c. 326	3-4-1959*	NDCC 45-05-01 to 45-09-15.
Ohio.	1949, p. 329	9-14-1949	R.C. §§ 1775.01-1775.42.

Jurisdiction	Laws	Effective Date	Statutory Citation
Oklahoma.	1955, p. 288	6-3-1955	54 Okl.St.Ann. §§ 201-244.
Oregon.	1939, c. 550	3-31-1939	ORS 68.010-68.650.
Pennsylvania. . .	1915, P.L. 18	7-1-1915	59 P.S. §§ 1-105.
Rhode Island. . .	1957, c. 74	10-1-1957	Gen.Laws 1956, §§ 7-12-12 to 7-12-55.
South Carolina. .	1950, p. 1841	2-13-1950	Code 1962, §§ 52-1 to 52-79.
South Dakota. . .	1923, c. 296	3-12-1923	Comp.Laws 1967, §§ 48-1-1 to 48-5-56.
Tennessee	1917, c. 140	7-1-1917	T.C.A. §§ 61-101 to 61-142.
Texas	1961, c. 158	1-1-1962	Vernon's Ann.Civ.St. art. 6132b.
Utah.	1921, c. 89	5-10-1921	U.C.A.1953, 48-1-1 to 48-1-40.
Vermont	1941, No. 146	3-31-1941	11 V.S.A §§ 1121-1335.
Virgin Islands. .	1957, Act, No. 160	9-1-1957	26 V.I.C. §§ 1-135.
Virginia.	1918, c. 365	7-1-1918	Code 1950, §§ 50-1 to 50-43.
Washington. . . .	1955, c. 15	2-8-1955	RCW 25.04.010-25.04.430.
West Virginia . .	1953, c. 139	3-13-1953	Code, 47-8A-1 to 47-8A-45.
Wisconsin	1915, c. 358	7-6-1915*	W.S.A. 178.01-178.39.
Wyoming	1917, c. 97	2-20-1917*	W.S.1957, §§ 17-195 to 17-237.

JURISDICTIONS ADOPTING THE UNIFORM LIMITED PARTNERSHIP ACT

(as of December, 1972)

Jurisdiction	Laws	Effective Date	Statutory Citation
Alabama. • • • • •	1971, No. 1512	1-1-1972	Code of Ala., Tit. 43, §§ 27(1) to 27 (31).
Alaska • • • • •	1917, c. 71	5-2-1917*	AS 32.10.010-32.10.290.
Arizona. • • • • •	1943, c. 60	3-19-1943*	A.R.S. §§ 29-301 to 29-329.
Arkansas • • • •	1953, Act 243	3-6-1953*	Ark.Stats. §§ 65-301 to 65-330.
California • • • •	1949, p. 668	5-23-1949*	West's Ann.Corp.Code, §§ 15501-15531.
Colorado • • • •	1931, c. 128	4-11-1931*	C.R.S. '53, 104-2-1 to 104-2-30.
Connecticut. • • •	1961, No. 79	5-3-1961*	C.G.S.A §§ 34-9 to 34-38.
Dist. of Columbia.	1962, P.L. 87-716, 76 Stat. 655	9-28-1962	D.C.C.E. § 41-401 et seq.
Florida. • • • •	1943, c. 21887	5-31-1943	F.S.A. §§ 620.01-620.32.
Georgia. • • • •	1952, p. 375	2-2-1952	Code, §§ 75-402 to 75-431.
Hawaii • • • • •	1943, Act 162	5-12-1943	R.L.H.1955, §§ 186-20 to 186-48.
Idaho. • • • • •	1919, c. 151	1-1-1920	I.C. §§ 53-201 to 53-232.

Jurisdiction	Laws	Effective Date	Statutory Citation
Illinois.	1917, p. 569	7-1-1917	S.H.A. ch. 106 1/2, §§ 44-73.
Indiana	1949, c. 121	9-10-1949	I.C.1971, 23-4-2-1 to 23-4-2-30.
Iowa.	40 Ex.G.A.H.F. 74, §§ 1-58	1924	I.C.A. §§ 545.1-545.58.
Kansas.	1967, c. 302	7-1-1967	K.S.A. 56-122 to 56-151.
Kentucky.	1970, c. 97		KRS 362.410 to 362.700.
Maine	1969, c. 324	9-1-1969	31 M.R.S.A. §§ 151 to 180.
Maryland.	1918, c. 280	4-10-1918*	Code 1957, art. 73, §§ 1-30.
Massachusetts	1923, c. 112	1-1-1924	M.G.L.A. c. 109 §§ 1-31.
Michigan.	1931, No. 110	5-18-1931*	M.C.L.A. §§ 449.201-449.231.
Minnesota	1919, c. 498	4-25-1919*	M.S.A. §§ 322.01-322.31.
Mississippi	1964, c. 271	4-22-1964*	Code 1942, §§ 5553-01 to 5554.5.
Missouri.	1947, Vol. 2, p. 311	5-11-1947*	V.A.M.S. §§ 359.010-359.290.
Montana	1947, c. 252	3-8-1947*	R.C.M.1947, §§ 63-701 to 63-911.
Nebraska.	1939, c. 87	3-17-1939*	R.R.S.1943, §§ 67-201 to 67-232.
Nevada.	1931, c. 73	7-1-1931	N.R.S. 88.010-88.310.

Jurisdiction	Laws	Effective Date	Statutory Citation
New Hampshire . .	1937, c. 101	5-12-1937*	RSA 305:1-305:30.
New Jersey . . .	1919, c. 211	4-15-1919	N.J.S.A. 42:2-1 to 42:2-30.
New Mexico . . .	1947, c. 120	3-19-1947*	1953 Comp. §§ 66-2-1 to 66-2-30.
New York	1922, c. 640	4-13-1922	McKinney's Partnership Law, §§ 90-119.
North Carolina .	1941, c. 251	3-15-1941	G.S. §§ 59-1 to 59-30.
North Dakota . .	1959, c. 326	3-4-1959*	NDCC 45-10-01 to 45-12-04.
Ohio	1957, p. 447	9-14-1957	R.C. §§ 1781.01-1781.27.
Oklahoma	1951, p. 144	5-29-1951*	54 Okl.St.Ann. §§ 141-171.
Oregon	1971, c. 594		
Pennsylvania . .	1917, P.L. 55	4-12-1917*	59 P.S. §§ 171-228.
Rhode Island . .	1930, c. 1571	4-1-1930	Gen.Laws 1956, §§ 7-13-1 to 7-13-31.
South Carolina .	1960, p. 1970	5-24-1960	Code 1962, §§ 52-101 to 52-128.
South Dakota . .	1925, c. 251	3-5-1925*	Comp.Laws 1967 §§ 48-6-1 to 48-6-64.
Tennessee. . . .	1919, c. 120	1-1-1920	T.C.A. §§ 61-201 to 61-230.
Texas.	1955, c. 133	4-30-1955	Vernon's Ann.Civ.St. art. 6132a.

Jurisdiction	Laws	Effective Date	Statutory Citation
Utah.	1921, c. 88	5-10-1921	U.C.A.1953, 48-2-1 to 48-2-27.
Vermont	1941, No. 145	3-31-1941	11 V.S.A. §§ 1391-1419.
Virgin Islands. .	1957, Act, No. 160	9-1-1957	26 V.I.C. §§ 201-228.
Virginia.	1918, c. 216	3-14-1918*	Code 1950, §§ 50-44 to 50-73.
Washington. . . .	1945, c. 92	3-15-1945*	RCWA 25.08.010-25.08.300.
West Virginia . .	1953, c. 140	90 days after 3-13-1953	Code, 47-9-1 to 47-9-30.
Wisconsin	1919, c. 449	6-28-1919*	W.S.A. 179.01-179.30.
Wyoming	1971, c. 86	7-1-1971	W.S.1957, §§ 17-263 to 17-293.

STATE STATUTORY PROVISIONS INCLUDING CORPORATIONS
FORMED FOR THE PURPOSE OF PRACTICING A PROFESSION
(effective July 1, 1972)

Alabama	Ala Code tit 10, § 21 (3)
Alaska	Alaska Stat § 10.05.003
Arizona	Ariz Rev Stat Ann § 10-121
Arkansas	Ark Stat Ann § 64-103
California	Cal Corp Code Ann §§ 119,300
Colorado	Colo Rev Stat Ann § 31-1-3
Connecticut	Conn Gen Stat Ann § 33-286
Delaware	Del Code Ann tit 8, § 101
District of Columbia	D.C. Code Ann § 29.903
Florida	Fla Stat Ann §§ 608.01, 608.03 (1
Georgia	Ga Code Ann § 22-201
Hawaii	Hawaii Rev Stat § 416-1
Idaho	Idaho Code Ann § 30-102
Illinois	Ill Rev Stat ch 32, §§ 157.3, 157
Indiana	Ind Ann Stat § 25-201
Iowa	Iowa Code Ann § 496A.3
Kansas	Kan Stat Ann 17-2706
Kentucky	Ky Rev Stat Ann § 271A.015
Louisiana	La Rev Stat § 12.22
Maine	Me Rev Stat Ann tit 13-A §§ 201, 401 as amended by Ch 565, L '72, eff 2-8-72

Maryland	Md Ann Code art 23, § 3
Massachusetts	Mass Gen Laws Ann ch 156B, § 3, as amended by Ch 392, L '69, eff 9-9-69
Michigan	Mich Comp Laws Ann §§ 450.1123, 450.1251 (1), enacted by P A 284, A '72, eff 1-1-73
Minnesota	Minn Stat Ann § 301.03
Mississippi	Miss Code Ann § 5309-03
Missouri	Ann Mo Stat §§ 351.020, 351.055 (8) (Vernon's)
Montana	Mont Rev Codes Ann § 15-2203
Nebraska	Neb Rev Stat § 21-2003, as amended by L B 1182, L '72, eff 7-6-72
Nevada	Nev Rev Stat §§ 78.020, 78.030
New Hampshire	N H Rev Stat Ann § 294.2
New Jersey	N J Stat Ann § 14A:2-1
New Mexico	N M Stat Ann § 51-24-3
New York	N Y Bus Corp Law § 201
North Carolina	N C Gen Stat § 55-5
North Dakota	N D Cent Code § 10-19-03
Ohio	Ohio Rev Code Ann § 17-01-03
Oklahoma	Okla Stat Ann tit 18, §§ 1.3, 1.9
Oregon	Ore Rev Stat § 57.025
Pennsylvania	Pa Stat Ann tit 15, § 1201
Rhode Island	R I Gen Laws Ann § 7-1.1-3, enacted by Ch 141, L '69, eff 1-2-70
South Carolina	S C Code §§ 12-12.1
South Dakota	S D Bus Corp Act § 3

Tennessee	Tenn Gen Corp Act § 3.01
Texas	Texas Bus Corp Act art 2.01 (Vernon
Utah	Utah Code Ann § 16-10-3
Vermont	Vt Stat Ann tit 11, § 1851, enacted by A 286, A ' 69, ratified by A 5 A '71, eff 7-1-71, as amended by A 51, A '71, eff 7-1-71
Virginia	Va Code Ann § 13.1-2(c)
Washington	Wash Rev Code § 23A-08.010
West Virginia	W Va Code Ann § 31-1-4
Wisconsin	Wis Stat Ann § 180.03
Wyoming	Wyo Stat § 17-36.3

STATE LAWS RELATING TO FRANCHISE REGULATION

Arkansas

1971 Acts of Ark., Act 252§2 approved Mar. 9, 1971, as amended H. B. 32, 1973.

California

Cal. Statutes & Code Amendments, Ch. 1400, 1970 Reg. Sess., amending Bus. & Prof. Code § 10177 and Corp. Code §§ 25019 and 25212, and adding Corp. Code, Tit. 4, Div. 5 §§ 31000-31516, approved Sept. 18, 1970, eff. Jan. 1, 1971.

Connecticut

Laws, 1972, P. A. 287, approved May 24, 1972.

Delaware

Del. Code, Tit. 6, Ch. 25, as amended Ch. 693, Vol. 57, Del. Laws, approved Sept. 7, 1970.

Florida

Fla. 1971 Reg. Sess., Ch. 71-61, approved May 24, 1971.

Kentucky

Ken. Rev. Stat. § 190.045-190.047 added by 1972 Acts, S. B. 84, approved March 17, 1972, eff. June 16, 1972.

Massachusetts

Gen. Laws Ch. 93B added by Acts, 1970, Ch. 814 § 1, approved Aug. 27, 1970, effective Jan. 1, 1971.

Gen. Laws, Ch. 93E added by Acts 1972, Ch. 772, approved July 17, 1972, eff. 90 days thereafter.

Mississippi

Miss. Code Anno., Temp. 1970 Supp. § 8071.7--01 et seq., effective July 1, 1970.

Nebraska

Leg. Bill 768, 1971 Sess. Laws, approved May 25, 1971, effective January 1, 1972.

Nevada

Nev. Rev. Stat., Ch. 482, as amended, Ch. 400, 55th Sess. Laws (1969).

New Jersey	N. J. Stat. Ann. §§ 56:10-1-- 56:10-12 as added by 1971 Reg. Sess.
	Laws, Ch. 356, approved and eff. Dec. 21, 1971.
New York	N. Y. Gen. Bus. Law, Art. 11A, as amended, N. Y. Laws 1970, Ch. 582.
Oklahoma	47 Okla. Stat. 1961 § 561 _et seq._, as amended, Ch. 197, Okla. Sess. Laws, 1970.
South Dakota	S. D. Laws 1969, Ch. 206.
	S. D. Laws 1971, Ch. 196.
Texas	Motor Vehicle Comm. Code, Vernon's Ann. Civ. Stat., Art. 4413 (36).
Utah	Utah Code Anno. §41-3-6 _et seq._
Virginia	Va. Code, Tit. 13.1, Ch. 8, 13.1-557--13.1-574, added by Va. Laws, 1972, Ch. 561.
Washington	RCW 19.100.010 _et seq._, Laws of 1971 ex. sess., Ch. 252, as amen. Laws, 1972, 1st ex. sess., Ch. 116.
West Virginia	W. Va. Code, Art. 16, Ch. 11 as amended by 1971 Acts, Ch. 9, passed Mar. 13, 1971.
Wisconsin	Wisc. Stat. Anno. Ch. 553 as added by Laws, 1971, Ch. 241.
	Wisc. Stat. Anno. Ch. 218. §218.01 (3) (a) (17), amended by Laws 1969, Ch. 500 § 30, eff. March 26, 1970.

PARTNERSHIP AGREEMENT

This agreement, entered into between James P. Reams, of Lawrence, Kansas, and Eldon J. Shields, of Lawrence, Kansas, this 15th day of November, 1973, at Lawrence, Kansas:

1. Name and Place of Business. The name of the partnership shall be REAMS HOLDINGS. The principal place of business shall be 207 Green Street, Lawrence, Kansas, and at such other localities within or without the state of Kansas as may be agreed upon by the partners.

2. Purpose of the Business. The partnership shall have as its purpose the investment of the partnership funds in stock, specifically 25 shares of Grand Trunk & Defunct Railway System, Ltd., and other lawful income producing investments and the distribution of any income derived therefrom to said partners.

3. Capital Contributions and Partnership Interests. Each partner shall contribute the sum of $250.00 on or before December 1, 1973. Each copartner shall have an equal, undivided one-half interest in all stock or other investments owned by the partnership. The profits shall be equally divided and each partner shall bear an equal share of all losses.

4. Control and Management. Both aforementioned partners are to have an equal voice in management of the partnership property. No partnership property shall be either purchased or sold without the consent of both partners.

It is further agreed between the said parties that neither partner shall have the right nor power to bind the partnership to wit: by loan, mortgage of other indenture, for any sum, without the consent of the other partner.

5. Sale or Desolution of the Partnership. Each of the above partners agrees and promises not to sell or convey his interest in said partnership unless the other partner consents. The partners further agree that at the death of either partner the surviving partner shall have the right to purchase the decedents interest in the partnership at a price to be determined by the surviving partner and the executor of the deceased partner's estate. Upon dissolution, either voluntary or involuntary, the assets shall be divided according

to the proportionate interests of the partners on the basis of their respective capital accounts as they stood on the date of such dissolution.

Signed the 26th day of November, 1973.

L. S. _____
James P. Reams

L. S. _____
Eldon J. Shields

ARTICLES OF INCORPORATION
A PROFESSIONAL CORPORATION

(Articles of incorporation under the laws of Florida for a
veterinary medicine practice)

Articles of Incorporation

Davidson, Llyod, and Reitman, Professional Association

The undersigned, subscribers to these Articles of Incorporation, natural persons cometent to contract, and veterinarians duly licensed to render services as such under
the laws of the State of Florida, hereby present these Articles for the formation of a corporation under The Professional Service Corporation Act, and other laws of the State
of Florida.

1. Name. The name of the Corporation is Davidson,
Llyod, and Reitman, Professional Association.

2. Nature of business. The general nature of the business to be transacted by the Corporation is:

(a) To engage in every phase and aspect of the business
of rendering the same professional services to the public
that a veterinarian, duly licensed under the laws of the
State of Florida, is authorized to render, but such professional services shall be rendered only through officers, em-

103

ployees, and agents who are duly licensed under the laws
of the State of Florida to practice veterinary medicine
therein.

(b) To invest the funds of the Corporation in real estate,
mortgages, stocks, bonds, or any other type of investment,
and to own real and personal property necessary for the
rendering of professional services.

(c) To do everything necessary and proper for the accomplishment of any of the purposes or the attaining of
any of the objects or the furtherance of any of the purposes
enumerated in these Articles of Incorporation or any amendment thereof, necessary or incidental to the protection
and benefit of the Corporation, and in general, either alone
or in association with other corporations, firms, or individuals, to carry on any lawful pursuit necessary or incidental to the accomplishment of the purposes or the attain-
ment of the objects or the furtherance of such purposes or
objects of the Corporation.

The foregoing paragraphs shall be construed as enumer-
ating both objects and purposes of the Corporation; and it
is hereby expressly provided that the foregoing enumeration
of specific purposes shall not be held to limit or restrict
in any manner the purposes of the Corporation otherwise
permitted by law.

3. Capital stock. The maximum number of shares of stock that the Corporation is authorized to have outstanding at any one time is 5,000 shares of common stock having a par value of $1 per share. None of the shares of the Corporation may be issued to anyone other than an individual duly licensed to practice veterinary medicine in the State of Florida.

4. Initial capital. The amount of capital with which the Corporation will begin business is $1,500.

5. Term of existence. The Corporation is to exist perpetually.

6. Address. The initial post office address of the principal office of the Corporation in the State of Florida is 101 Shelard Street, Winterhaven, Florida. The Board of Directors may from time to time move the principal office to any other address in the State of Florida.

7. Directors. The business of the Corporation shall be managed by its Board of Directors. The number of directors constituting the entire Board shall not be less than three; and subject to such minimum may be increased or decreased from time to tome by amendment of the Bylaws in a manner not prohibited by law. Until so changed the number shall be three.

105

8.   Initial directors. The names and street addresses of the members of the first Board of Directors are:

Name	Address
James Davidson	200 Lawrence St.
	Winterhaven, Florida
Ralph Llyod	113 Virginia Circle
	Winterhaven, Florida
Joseph Reitman	5611 Early St.
	Winterhaven, Florida

9.   Subscribers. The names and street addresses of each person signing the Articles of Incorporation as a subscriber, each of whom is a veterinarian, duly licensed under the laws of the State of Florida to render services as such, the number of shares of stock each agrees to take, and the value of the consideration therefor are:

Name	Address	Number of Shares	Consideration
James Davidson	200 Lawrence St.	500	$500
Ralph Llyod	113 Virginia Circle	500	$500
Joseph Reitman	5611 Early St.	500	$500
	Winterhaven, Florida		

10.   Voting trusts. No stockholder of the Corporation shall enter into a voting trust agreement or any other type

of agreement vesting in another person the authority to
exercise the voting power of any or all of his shares.

11. Cumulative voting for directors. At all elections
of directors of the Corporation, each stockholder shall be
entitled to as many votes as shall equal the number of votes
which (except for these provisions as to cumulative voting)
he would be entitled to cast for the election of directors with
respect to his shares of stock multiplied by the number of
directors to be elected, and he may cast all such votes for
a single director, or may distribute them among the number
to be voted for, or any two or more of them, as he may see
fit.

12. Contracts. No contract or other transaction between
the Corporation and any other corporation shall be affected
by the fact that any director of the Corporation is interested
in, or is a director or officer of, such other corporation, and
any director, individually or jointly, may be a party to, or
may be interested in, any contract or transaction of the Corporation or in which the Corporation is interested; and no
contract or other transaction of the Corporation with any
person, firm, or corporation shall be affected by the fact
that any director of the Corporation is a party in any
way connected with such person, firm, or corporation, and
every person who may become a director of the Corporation is hereby relieved from any liability that might other-

wise exist from contracting with the Corporation for the
benefit of himself or any firm, association, or corporation
in which he may be in any way interested.

13. Removal of directors. Any director of the Corporation may be removed at any annual or special meeting of
the stockholders by the same vote as that required to elect
a director.

14. Restraint on alienation of shares. The stockholders
of the Corporation shall have the power to include in the
Bylaws, adopted by a two-thirds majority of the stockholders of the Corporation, any regulatory or restrictive
provisions regarding the proposed sale, transfer, or other
disposition of any of the outstanding stock of the Corporation by any of its stockholders, or in the event of the death
of any of its stockholders. The manner and form, as well
as the relevant terms, conditions, and details thereof, shall
be determined by the stockholders of the Corporation; provided, however, that such regulatory or restrictive provisions
shall not affect the rights of third parties without actual
notice thereof, unless the existence of such provisions shall
be plainly written upon the certificate evidencing the ownership of such stock. No stockholder of the Corporation may
sell or transfer his stock therein except to another individual
who is eligible to be a stockholder of the Corporation, and
such sale or transfer may be made only after the same shall

have been approved at a stockholders' meeting specially called for such purpose. If any stockholder shall become legally disqualified to practice veterinary medicine in the State of Florida, or be elected to a public office, or accept employment that places restrictions or limitations upon his continuous rendering of such professional services, such stockholder's shares of stock shall immediately become subject to purchase by the Corporation in accordance with the Bylaws adopted by the stockholders.

15. Additional corporate powers. In furtherance and not in limitation of the general powers conferred by the laws of the State of Florida and of the purposes and objects hereinabove stated, the Corporation shall have all the following powers:

(a) To enter into, or become a partner in, any arrangement for sharing profits, union of interest, or cooperation, joint venture, or otherwise, with any person, firm, or corporation for the purpose of carrying on any business which the Corporation has the direct or incidental authority to pursue.

(b) To deny to the holders of the common stock of the Corporation any preemptive right to purchase or subscribe to any such stock.

(c) At its option, to purchase and acquire any or all of its stock owned and held by any such stockholder as should desire to sell, transfer, or otherwise dispose of his stock in accordance with the Bylaws adopted by the stockholders of the Corporation setting forth the terms and conditions of such purchase; provided, however, that the capital of the Corporation is not impaired.

(d) At its option, to purchase and acquire the stock owned and held by any stockholder who dies, in accordance with the Bylaws adopted by the stockholders of the Corporation setting forth the terms and conditions of such purchase; provided, however, that the capital of the Corporation is not impaired.

(e) To enter into, for the benefit of its employees, one or more of the following: (1) a pension plan, (2) a profit-sharing plan, (3) a stock bonus plan, (4) a thrift and savings plan, (5) a restricted stock option plan, or (6) other retirement or incentive compensation plans.

16. Amendment. These Articles of Incorporation may be amended in the manner provided by law. Every amendment shall be approved by the Board of Directors, proposed by them to the stockholders, and approved at a stock- holers' meeting by a majority of the stock entitled to vote thereon, unless all the directors and all the stockholders sign a written statement manifesting their intention that a

certain amendment of these Articles of Incorporation be made. All rights of stockholders are subject to this reservation.

In witness whereof we the subscribers have executed these Articles of Incorporation this 30th day of June, 1971.

. . . .
James Davidson

. . . .
Ralph Llyod

. . . .
Joseph Reitman

[Acknowledgments

by notary]

STOCKHOLDERS' AGREEMENT

THIS AGREEMENT made as of the 15th day of September, 1970, between John Jones of 22 Main Street, Portchester, New York, and Tom Smith of 11 Lincoln Road, New York, N. Y. (hereinafter sometimes referred to as the "shareholders").

W I T N E S S E T H :

WHEREAS, the shareholders have caused SUNKIST CLEANERS, INC., to be organized as a corporation under the Laws of the State of New York, and have agreed that it shall be financed and capitalized and its business conducted subject to the provisions of this agreement.

NOW, THEREFORE, in consideration of the mutual covenants herein contained, it is agreed:

(1) The shareholders each hereby subscribe for and agree to purchase five (5) shares each of the capital stock of the corporation at $50.00 per share. These shares shall be issued and paid for within five (5) days after the organization of the corporation.

(2) The shareholders each hereby agree to loan to the

corporation the sum of Five Thousand ($5,000.) Dollars, to
be used for the purposes of the business of the corporation,
such loan to be repaid at the convenience of the corporation, with interest thereon at six (6%) per cent per annum.

(3)   The corporation shall employ John Jones and Tom
Smith each at a salary of One Hundred and Fifty ($150.00)
Dollars per week. John Jones and Tom Smith each agree to
accept such employment, to devote their full time and best
efforts to the business of the corporation, and not to be
interested in or engage in any other competing business,
directly or indirectly. Such salary shall be subject to increase or decrease and the term of employment of John Jones
and Tom Smith may be terminated only by vote of the Board
of Directors of the corporation in accordance with the provisions contained in the Certificate of Incorporation.

(4)   In the event that either John Jones or Tom Smith
shall at any time, for any reason whatsoever, leave the
employ of the corporation or cease to be actively engaged
in the business of the corporation, all of the shares owned
by such stockholder shall be offered for sale to the other
shareholder, who is hereby given an option for a period
of thirty (30) days from the date on which such employment
or activity shall terminate, to purchase all of such shares
at a price equal to the book value thereof. Book value of
shares shall be computed from the books of the corporation

113

maintained by its regular accountant in accordance with generally accepted principles of accounting. The option here given shall relate to only all of such shares of the offering shareholder, and the purchasing shareholder shall not have the right to purchase only part thereof. If the aforesaid offer is accepted, notwithstanding any of the foregoing provisions of this paragraph, the selling shareholder shall receive from the purchasing shareholder, not less than the value of his investment in the corporation plus the amount of any unpaid loan theretofore made by the selling shareholder to the corporation, with appropriate interest thereon to the date of purchase. Payments to be made under this paragraph shall be made as follows: one-third (1/3) upon the acceptance of the offer; one-third (1/3) three (3) months thereafter; and the final one-third (1/3) six (6) months thereafter. Title to the shares shall pass to the purchaser only upon the completion of all payments. After the payment of the first one-third (1/3) installment, the retiring shareholder shall hold such shares only as security for payment of the remaining installments, and the purchaser shall have the sole right to vote the shares and to collect all dividends and other distributions thereon. Upon payment of the last installment, the shares shall be transferred of record to the purchaser.

(5) Each of the shareholders expressly agrees not to

transfer, sell, assign, pledge or otherwise in any manner
dispose of or encumber any of his shares unless and until
he shall have offered to sell all of his shares to the other
shareholder at a price to be computed and to be paid as
specified in paragraph "(4)" above. Such offer shall be
made in writing and shall continue for thirty (30) days
from the date thereof.

(6) All stock certificates issued by the corporation
shall have marked on the face thereof "Subject to provisions of stockholders agreement dated September 15, 1951,
restricting transfer." No dividend shall be paid on any
shares transferred, pledged, assigned or encumbered in
breach of this agreement.

(7) Upon the death of any shareholder who is also an
employee, his salary shall be paid to his widow or next of
kin for eight (8) weeks following such death. If any shareholder shall become physically incapacitated and unable
to attend to his duties as an employee of the corporation,
he shall continue to receive his full salary (less the sum
required to employ a substitute in his place) for a period
of four (4) months after the commencement of such incapacity.
In the event of the death, or incapacity of any shareholder-
employee for more than four (4) months, the other shareholder
shall have the option, for thirty (30) days after such death
or expiration of said four (4) month period, to purchase his

shares at the price and on the terms provided for in paragraph "(4)" hereof. The life of each shareholder shall be insured for the benefit of the other shareholder for Five Thousand ($5,000.) Dollars, or for such other amount as the shareholders may jointly agree upon. If the proceeds of such insurance payable to any shareholder are equal to at least fifty (50%) per cent of the purchase price of the stock of the deceased shareholder as computed in accordance with the provisions of paragraph "(4)", such shareholder agrees that he will exercise his option to purchase all of the shares from the estate of the deceased shareholder as herein provided. Upon the receipt of any such proceeds, any then remaining unpaid installments of such purchase price shall be prepaid by the purchaser, to at least the extent of such proceeds.

(8) Each shareholder agrees, so long as he shall remain a shareholder, to vote his shares for the election of the following four (4) persons as Directors of the corporation:

> John Jones,
> Mary Jones (or such other person as is des-
>   ignated by John Jones),
> Tom Smith, and
> Dick Smith (or such other person as is desig-
>   nated by Tom Smith).

and generally to so vote at directors and stockholders meeting of the corporation as to carry out and make effective all the terms and provisions of this agreement.

(9) So long as they are faithful in the performance of their duties, the following persons shall be supported by the shareholders for election to offices of the corporation:

President and Treasurer-- John Jones

Vice President and Secretary-- Tom Smith

(10) All disputes, differences and controversies arising under and in connection with this agreement shall be settled and finally determined by arbitration in the City of New York according to the rules of the American Arbitration Association now in force or hereafter adopted.

(11) This agreement shall continue in force during the entire period of the life of the corporation.

(12) This agreement and all provisions hereof shall enure to the benefit of and shall be binding upon the heirs, executors, legal representatives, next of kin, transferees and assigns of the parties hereto.

(13) If for any reason any provision hereof shall be

inoperative, the validity and effect of all other provisions hereof shall not be affected thereby.

(14) No modification or waiver of any provision of this agreement shall be valid unless in writing signed by all of the parties hereto.

IN WITNESS WHEREOF, the parties have hereunto set their hands and seals the day and year first above written.

_____
JOHN JONES

_____
TOM SMITH

Confirmed and Agreed to:
SUNKIST CLEANERS, INC.

_____
President

Attest:

_____
Secretary

Silent partner, 24

Small Business Act of 1953, 57

Small Business Administration, 55; creation of, 56; eligibility for assistance, 60; financial assistance by, 57, 60; investment assistance by, 59; lease guarantee program, 65; loan programs, 60; management assistance by, 58, 71; minority assistance, 66; procurement assistance, 69; publications, 71; purposes of, 57; research by, 59; set-aside contracts, 69; Small Business Investment Companies, 68; surety band program, 65

Small business corporation, defined, 4

Small Business Investment Act of 1958, 57

Small Defense Plants Administration, 55

Small War Plants Corporation, 55

Social Security laws, 75

Sole proprietorship, 5; advantages, 5; disadvantages, 5; ease of incorporation, 5; profits, 5; taxation of, 73

Statistical Abstract of the United States, 1, 4

Stockholder, 3, 13, 16; taxation of, 74

Stockholder agreements, 21, 115; advantages, 21; election of officers, 24; profits, 23; stock purchase, 25; termination of business, 25

Taxation, 3; corporations, 13, 74; double taxation, 4, 13, 74; employer witholding obligations, 74; excise tax, 75; federal taxes, 74; partnership, 7, 74; personal property, 75; prices, effect on, 82; professional corporations, 17; sole proprietorship, 5, 74; state taxes, 74; Subchapter S, 4

Technical Amendment Act of 1958, 4

Termination of business, 25

Trade-marks, 30, 47; confusion of, 45, 48; defined, 47; selection of, 48; U.S. Patent Office, 47, 48

Trade names, 45; purchase of, 43; restrictions, 46

Unemployment insurance, 76

Unfair competition, law of, 79, 80

Uniform Commercial Code, 42, 83

Uniform Consumer Credit Code, 79, 83

Uniform Limited Partnership Act, 9, 92

Uniform Partnership Act, 6, 89

United States Department of Commerce, 51

United States Government Manual, 78

United States Government Purchasing and Sales Directory, 71

United States Patent Office, 47, 48

Washington, George, 1

Wholesome Meat Act of 1967, 58, 64

Wholesome Poultry Products Act of 1967, 58, 64

Workmen's Compensation Insurance 77

121